Disney's

WONDERFUL WORLD OF KNOWLEDGE

YEAR BOOK 1987

Disney's

Wonderful World of Knowledge

YEAR BOOK 1987

GROLIER ENTERPRISES, INC.
Danbury, Connecticut

ROBERT B. CLARKE   *Publisher*

FERN L. MAMBERG   *Executive Editor*

MICHÈLE A. McLEAN   *Art Director*

MARGARET M. FINA   *Production Manager*

ISBN 0-7172-8195-7
The Library of Congress Catalog Card Number: 78-66149

Text on pages 32-35, 56-59, 84-87, 108-111,
and all Disney character illustrations
Copyright © 1987, The Walt Disney Company

COPYRIGHT © 1987 BY

Copyright © in Canada 1987 BY GROLIER LIMITED

PRINTED IN THE UNITED STATES OF AMERICA

Grolier Enterprises Inc. offers a varied
selection of both adult and children's book
racks. For details on ordering, please write
to: Grolier Enterprises Inc., Sherman Turnpike,
Danbury, CT 06816, Attn: Premium Department.

CONTENTS

1986 AT A GLANCE

JANUARY 7. President Ronald Reagan announced that the United States would sever economic ties with Libya. He also ordered all Americans living in Libya to leave immediately. These actions were in response to Libyan support for international terrorism, which Reagan called "a threat to the national security and foreign policy of the United States."

JANUARY 20. France and Britain announced that they would build two rail tunnels under the English Channel. The proposed "chunnel," to be completed in 1993, would be 30 miles (48 kilometers) long. It would run between Dover, England, and Calais, France. One tunnel would be for high-speed trains; the second would be for special trains designed to carry cars and buses.

JANUARY 28. A little over a minute after liftoff, the space shuttle *Challenger* exploded, killing all seven astronauts aboard. It was the worst disaster in U.S. space history. The crew consisted of Gregory B. Jarvis, Ronald E. McNair, Ellison S. Onizuka, Judith A. Resnik, Francis R. Scobee, Michael J. Smith, and Christa McAuliffe—a high school teacher from New Hampshire who was to have been the first "ordinary" citizen in space.

JANUARY 29. Richard E. Lyng was named U.S. Secretary of Agriculture, to succeed John R. Block.

FEBRUARY 20. The Soviet Union launched the space station Mir (for "peace") into orbit around Earth. The station was designed as the first step in the creation of a permanently manned space research complex. Mir is more sophisticated than previous stations, and it has six docking ports for visiting spacecraft.

APRIL 5. A bomb exploded in a discotheque in West Berlin, killing two people, including an American soldier, and wounding 230 others. The U.S. government later said that it had "irrefutable proof" of Libyan involvement in the bombing.

APRIL 14. U.S. planes bombed "terrorist-related targets" in the Libyan cities of Tripoli and Benghazi. President Ronald Reagan said the attack was in retaliation for the April 5 discotheque bombing in West Berlin and also for the "reign of terror" that Libyan leader Muammar el-Qaddafi had launched against the United States. The U.S. bombing killed at least 15 people and wounded 60 others. One U.S. plane was downed and its two crew members killed.

APRIL 26. Explosions ripped through the Soviet Union's Chernobyl nuclear power plant, igniting fires, crippling a nuclear reactor, and spewing radioactive material into the atmosphere. The accident was the worst in the history of nuclear power. Countries around the world strongly criticized the Soviets for having withheld information about the disaster for almost two days, until Sweden detected radioactivity in the atmosphere. About 300 people living near the power plant were injured, and at least 31 people died—most from radiation and burns. Radioactivity from the accident was carried around the globe by high-level winds. In the Soviet countryside and in several nearby European countries, there were fears that the radiation had contaminated crops, milk, and other farm produce. The levels were considered too low to be hazardous in North America.

MAY 25. Some 5,000,000 people joined hands to participate in Hands Across America, a fund-raising event to help the hungry and homeless in the United States. The chain of people, most of whom contributed money to the cause, reached from New York to California, with only a few gaps in the line (in the Arizona desert, for example). Other people, in states not on the route, joined hands to form smaller, local chains.

JUNE 17. Warren E. Burger, Chief Justice of the U.S. Supreme Court since 1969, announced that he would retire. Associate Justice William H. Rehnquist, a member of the Supreme Court since 1971, was named to succeed Burger. Antonin Scalia, a judge of the Court of Appeals for the District of Columbia, was named to succeed Rehnquist as Associate Justice.

JULY 4. Festive events that included a parade of sailing ships in New York Harbor and the biggest fireworks display in U.S. history marked the 100th birthday of the Statue of Liberty—America's monument that symbolizes the concepts of hope and freedom.
■ American Greg LeMond became the first non-European cyclist to win the Tour de France—the world's most important bicycle race.

AUGUST 13. It was reported that fossil bones found in western Texas may be the remains of the world's earliest birds. The 225,000,000-year-old fossils were from birds that scientists have named *Protoavis* (for "first bird"). The bones were dug out of ancient mud in 1984, and they belonged to two birds the size of crows. The discovery supported the theory that birds developed from reptiles—because the ancient birds were like dinosaurs in some ways.

AUGUST 21. In northwest Cameroon, a cloud of toxic gases escaped from a lake in a volcanic crater. More than 1,500 people were killed as the poisonous fumes from Lake Nios spread over four mountain villages. Poisonous gases are often present in the vapors released by volcanoes, even without a major volcanic eruption. These gases are usually trapped at the bottom of crater lakes. But some unexplained occurrence in Lake Nios made the gases shoot up to the surface, explode, and fill the air.

SEPTEMBER 5. Four Arab terrorists seized a Pan American jet in Karachi, Pakistan. The airplane carried 389 passengers and crew members. After holding the plane on the ground for sixteen hours, the gunmen panicked when its generator ran out of fuel and the lights dimmed. They herded the passengers to the middle of the plane, opened fire, and threw hand grenades at them. Some passengers began to escape through emergency doors, and the terrorists were then captured by Pakistani commandos who stormed the plane. Twenty-one people, including two Americans, were killed.

SEPTEMBER 6. In Istanbul, Turkey, two Arab terrorists attacked worshippers at a synagogue during the morning Sabbath service, killing at least 21 people. The terrorists were killed when one of their grenades exploded.

SEPTEMBER 23. The U.S. House of Representatives voted to make the rose America's national flower. (The Senate had passed the resolution in 1985.) The action ended a debate that went back to the late 1800's. Over the years, people had proposed many flowers as the "national floral emblem"—including the dogwood, the marigold, the mountain laurel, and the corn tassel.

OCTOBER 2.   As a protest against South Africa's racial policy of apartheid, the U.S. Congress imposed strong economic sanctions on the country. In doing so, Congress overrode President Ronald Reagan, who had earlier vetoed the bill. The new law banned American loans to and investments in South Africa; halted imports of South African iron, steel, coal, uranium, textiles, and agricultural products; and ended landing rights for South African Airways in the United States.

OCTOBER 12.   U.S. President Ronald Reagan and Soviet leader Mikhail Gorbachev completed two days of talks in Reykjavik, Iceland. Their discussions focused on arms-control issues, but no agreements were reached.

OCTOBER 22.   The most sweeping revision of U.S. income tax laws since the 1940's was signed into law by President Ronald Reagan. The new law would eliminate taxes for low-income groups and reduce taxes for many other taxpayers. At the same time, it would raise taxes for businesses and end many "tax shelters" that had allowed wealthy people to pay less. The provisions of the new tax law were to be phased in over a four-year period.

NOVEMBER 1.   Tons of poisonous chemicals spilled into the Rhine River when a fire destroyed a chemical storage building near Basel, Switzerland. The chemicals endangered drinking-water supplies and killed hundreds of thousands of fish. The four countries through which the Rhine flows—Switzerland, France, West Germany, and the Netherlands—closed plants that process Rhine water for drinking, banned fishing in the river, and took steps to prevent the polluted water from seeping into streams and underground water reserves.

DECEMBER 23.   Richard Rutan and Jeana Yeager, two pilots from California, ended a nine-day flight in their *Voyager* airplane and set a new record: They flew nonstop around the world without refueling, covering a distance of 25,012 miles (40,253 kilometers). They were the first people to circle the globe on a single load of fuel. *Voyager* was specially designed for record-breaking flights. It was built almost entirely of lightweight plastics and stiffened paper, and it weighed less than a compact car. But it could carry up to five time its own weight, and most of what it carried was fuel (even its long, hollow wings were filled with fuel). To save weight, the cockpit was as small as possible—not much bigger than a bathtub. While one pilot sat halfway up to fly the plane, the other had to lie down. Two propellers, fore and aft, pushed and pulled *Voyager* to a top speed of 100 miles (161 kilometers) an hour.

WHAT'S IN A NAME?

If you're like most people, you probably have several names: a first name, perhaps a middle name, and a last name (or surname). Your first name and your middle name were given to you at birth by your parents. Your surname is the same as theirs. But have you ever wondered how your family got its surname?

People didn't always have surnames. In fact, there are still a few places in the world where they don't. If there are only a few people in a village, first names are enough to tell them apart. But when there are more people, first names can be confusing—there may be ten, twenty, or two hundred Johns in a town. Surnames help distinguish one from the other.

Family names go back more than 2,000 years in China and in India. In many Western countries, however, surnames are more recent. In England, for example, surnames weren't used until after the Norman Conquest, in 1066. And in England and most other countries, people chose (or were given) their surnames in several different ways.

PATRONYMICS

One of the most common types of surnames is the patronymic—a name formed from the first name of a person's father or other male ancestor. For example, Peter the son of John became Peter Johnson. And the common surname Jones is an English-Welsh name that means "the son of Jone."

Patronymics are found in many countries and in many different languages. In Scotland and parts of Ireland, the prefixes *Mc* and *Mac* were used to mean "son of." McArthur, then, was the son of Arthur. Elsewhere in Ireland, *Fitz* was used in the same way, as in FitzGerald. The prefix *O'* had a looser meaning, "descendant of." In Germany, the suffix *sohn* was used—Mendelsohn, the son of Mendel. The Slavic languages also used suffixes—*vitch, off,* and *kin*. The son of Ivan might be Ivanovitch or Ivanoff.

You might wonder why you don't hear of names that mean "daughter of." The reason is that in most countries, women take their husbands' surnames when they marry. And the children carry the father's name, too. Thus a name that meant "daughter of" wouldn't survive even one generation. Although more women are choosing to keep their own names when they marry, the father's name is still the one carried by most children.

In some places, however, "daughter of"

John Swift   John Armstrong   John Merriman   John Lowe   John Beard

is used. In Iceland, all last names are formed from the father's first name—by adding *son* for a boy or *dottir* for a girl. Sveinn Asgeirsson's son Björn would be Björn Sveinnsson, and his daughter Vigdis would be Vigdis Sveinnsdottir. When Björn marries, his children would carry the last names Björnsson and Björnsdottir. When Vigdis marries, she would keep her surname. But her children's surname would be formed from her husband's first name. Icelanders usually call each other by their first names. And to avoid confusion, their telephone directories list people's occupations as well as names and addresses.

Hispanic names combine the father's and mother's names—Roberto Rodriguez López would be the son of a man named Rodriguez who married a woman named López. But when Roberto marries and has children, he will combine his father's name—Rodriguez—with his wife's name to form his children's names. López won't be carried on.

NAMES FROM TRADE

Some people carry names that show their ancestors' jobs or positions in society. If your name is Cooper, for example, you can bet that somewhere in your family history there was a man who made barrels for a living. In the same way, a man named Harold who made leather became Harold Tanner and passed on the name to his children. Some other common names that developed in this way are Baker, Barber, Carpenter, Carter, Clark (for clerk), Cook, Dyer, Hunter, Shepherd, Stewart (for steward), Taylor, Thatcher, and Weaver.

The most common English name of all—Smith—refers to the blacksmith, who forged tools and weapons and shod horses. This job was so essential that there was a blacksmith in every village. And because war and fighting were everyday occurrences during the Middle Ages, Archer, Fletcher (arrow maker), and Armour are common names today. Other names show the position an ancestor held in society—Baron, Knight, Chamberlain, Butler.

Similar names appear in many other languages. Smith, for example, is Schmidt in German, Ferrari in Italian, Herrera in Spanish, Kowalski in Polish, Kovar in Czech, and Seppanen in Finnish. Taylor is Schneider in German, Portnoy in Russian, and Kravitz in Polish. Some other common German names are Bauer (farmer) and Metzger (butcher). The Hebrew name Cohen originally referred to a prince or a priest.

NAMES FROM NICKNAMES

Suppose you've gone back in time to a medieval village to look for a man named John. There are five Johns in this village, so how will the villagers know which one you want? That's easy—you'll describe him. He's the John who has the beard, or the one who's so short. Perhaps he's always cheerful, or maybe he has strong arms or runs very fast.

Before surnames were common, people often went by nicknames that were based on physical or personality characteristics. And in many cases, these nicknames were shortened into real surnames that stuck with the people and their families. John with the beard became John Beard. The short John

Christopher
Wren
(architect)

Florence
Nightingale
(nurse)

John
Jay
(jurist)

Peter
Finch
(actor)

Thomas Love
Peacock
(poet)

Lynn
Swann
(football player)

became John Lowe. John who always smiled became John Merriman. John who ran fast became John Swift, while he of the strong arms became John Armstrong.

There are similar names in other languages. The Irish name Sullivan, for example, originally meant "black-eyed." The Russian name Tolstoy meant "fat." Today these names usually have nothing to do with the physical characteristics or personalities of their bearers. You may know a Sullivan with blue eyes, a Lowe who's six feet tall, or a Merriman who's always sad. But you can be certain that at sometime in their family histories, they had ancestors who lived up to their names.

NATURE NAMES

Many people took their surnames from the world around them—from the places where they lived or from some aspect of nature. Many English names, for example, were originally the names of towns and other

places in England: Bradford, Bristol, Chester, Lincoln, Sherwood. The ancestors of a person named Maynard probably lived in the duchy of Maine, a region of France.

Other names came from geographical features. Henry who lived on the hill became Henry Hill, while Walter who lived near a ford of a river became Walter Ford. Some other names formed the same way are Brook, Field, Grove, Lake, Rivers, Stiles, Wells, and Woods.

Common plants were also sources for names—Rice and Oates, for example. So were the names of birds and other animals—Dove, Finch, Fish, Partridge, and Woodcock in English; Adler (eagle) and Krebs (crabs) in German. Some people, however, took these names not because they were nature lovers, but for another reason: Before the 1800's, most people couldn't read. So every merchant put an easily recognized symbol (whether it had to do with his business or not) on the signboard in front of his shop. The merchants became known by their symbols (birds, flowers, angels), and the symbols became their surnames. In this way a German merchant who hung a picture of a star outside his shop acquired the name Stern—the German word for star.

NAMES BY CHANCE AND CHOICE

People didn't always acquire their surnames willingly. Sometimes the government ordered them to take names. In the mid-1400's, when England ruled Ireland, the English king Edward IV ordered all the Irish to take English surnames. They were allowed to choose the name of a place (such as Cork or Kinsale), the title of a job or occupation, or a color such as white, black, or brown.

In the early 1800's, the Russian czar Alexander I ordered all Russian Jews to take surnames. The officials in charge of assigning the new names saw a chance to make some money. They granted pleasant-sounding names only on payment of a big bribe; those who couldn't pay got less attractive names like Lumpe and Schmaltz.

Sometimes governments restricted what surnames could be used. In ancient China, the emperor decreed that all family names should be drawn from the text of a certain sacred poem. Because that limited the choice, many Chinese families have the same name. Among the most popular are Chang ("drawn bow"), Wang ("prince")

and Li ("plum"). Unlike people in Western countries, the Chinese give their family names ahead of their individual names. A child named Wei born to the Chang family would be called Chang Wei.

Many surnames have changed over the centuries—either by accident or because their bearers wanted to change them. Spellings weren't set until the 1800's, when dictionaries became popular, so different spellings produced many variations in names. William Shakespeare's name, for example, was spelled 83 different ways.

In the United States, immigration produced many name changes. This happened in two ways. Sometimes immigrants changed their names by choice because having a foreign-sounding name made it harder to find a job and a place to live. And sometimes immigration officials were responsible for the changes—they couldn't understand or spell a newcomer's correct name, so they wrote down any English name that sounded similar.

Today there are over 1,000,000 different names in the United States, and they originated in countries all over the world. But there's still a lot of duplication—more than 2,000,000 Smiths, for example. So if you're looking for Mary Smith, you may have to add something to her name—"Mary Smith who lives on the hill," or "the smart Mary Smith," or "Mary Smith who runs fast."

Honeybee

BEE MY LOVE

Few things are as lovely as flowers, with their bright colors, delicate forms, and soft scents. But if it weren't for animals, most flowers wouldn't exist. The reason is that animals help flowering plants reproduce.

Flowering plants form seeds by combining male and female cells, through a process called pollination. The reproductive parts are in the flowers. At the center of the flower is a vase-shaped post called the pistil. This is the female part, and it's where the ovules, or eggs, are produced.

Around the pistil is a ring of slender stalks called stamens. These are the male parts,

and it's where the pollen develops. When the pollen grains are ripe, they must be transferred from stamen to pistil. When this occurs, the pollen grains fertilize the ovules, which then develop into the seeds that will form new plants.

If pollen is transferred from the stamen to the pistil of the same flower, the process is called self-pollination. But not every plant can fertilize itself. In many plant species, some flowers contain only pistils and others have only stamens. Even when flowers contain both stamens and pistils, they often can't self-pollinate—because this usually

Hummingbird

Moth

isn't the best method of reproduction. Cross-pollination, which combines the pollen of one plant with the ovules of another plant of the same kind, mixes the genetic material of the two plants. The result is usually stronger plants and better fruit.

And this is where animals help—they carry the pollen from one plant to another. They don't know they're helping. Usually they go to the flowers to drink the sweet nectar inside or to eat the pollen itself. But in the process, their bodies pick up a few grains of pollen, which are then carried to the next flower they visit.

Bees are the most famous pollinators—and the busiest, visiting flower after flower after flower. You'll often see hives of hon-eybees set beneath the trees in orchards, placed there specifically so that the bees will pollinate the fruit trees. Beetles, moths, and butterflies are other pollinating insects.

Some birds help, too—tiny hummingbirds hover in the air as they drink the nectar from a flower, and then dart off to the next. There are even small mammals that help pollinate flowers. They include bats and the tiny Australian honey possum.

These animals and others like them are so important to plants that they are actually the reason that flowers even exist. The bright petals, wonderful scents, and sweet-tasting nectar of flowers are there for one purpose: to attract animals that will help the plant reproduce.

Honey possum

TALES OF FAIRIES

Up the airy mountain,
Down the rushy glen,
We daren't go a-hunting,
For fear of little men.
William Allingham

The grass bends, and the leaves rustle with a soft sigh. A passing breeze, you say, and dismiss it without a second thought. But could it have been something else—something magical and mysterious?

In olden days, the rustling leaves might have been given a different explanation: A troop of fairies, invisible but real all the same, had passed by. Fairies, so it was believed, were magical beings of the woods and hills. They lived in a world that existed side by side with ours but wasn't the same. Sometimes the two worlds would cross. A lonely traveler might see a fairy castle rising from the mist, or catch a glimpse of a fairy ring—a lush green circle in a meadow or forest where the fairies danced. But when the traveler arrived at the scene, every trace of the sight would have vanished.

FAIRY FOLK

Stories of fairies are common in the British Isles and northern Europe. The word "fairy" can be traced back to the Old French word *feer,* to enchant, and to the Latin word *fatum,* or fate. And indeed, fairies had both the power of enchantment and the ability to see into the future.

Fairies were also known as elves, from the Scandinavian word *alfar*. The terms are confusing because both have been used for a great variety of strange and mythical beings—from tall, beautiful maidens who can enchant ordinary men with a mere glance to tiny blackened gnomes who inhabit hearths and play mischievous pranks around the house. But fairies and elves as we usually think of them can be divided into two groups.

The oldest tales tell of fairies who were tall and slender, graceful and fair. Their kingdoms were hidden—beneath lakes, inside the hollow hills (burial mounds left by early people), and on far-off magical islands shrouded in mist. Later tales describe fairies as little people—small enough to wear a flower for a cap or use a toadstool as a seat. A few, the tales say, even had wings and flitted about like insects. Some of the Scandinavian elves were said to be evil fairies whose realms were underground. But most stories present fairies as neither good nor evil. Fairies might use their powers to help humans. But they were quick to take offense, and once offended they were more likely to use their powers for harm.

For this reason, people who believed in these creatures seldom called them by name; to use a name without its owner's permission was, in times gone by, a great offense. Instead, it was safer to refer to them as the Fairy Folk, the Good People, the Gentry, the Blessed Court, the Mothers' Blessing.

STANDING TALL

How did tales of fairies arise? Some people think they began far back in history, when early inhabitants of an area were driven out by conquerors. The defeated people "went underground"—they lived hidden in caves and forests and went about secretly at night. The conquerors knew they were there, though. Every so often, one would be seen. Or a bit of food or a tool carelessly left lying around would disappear, taken by the silent folk.

The tall fairies of the stories were like humans in some ways. They were ruled by beautiful kings and queens, and they enjoyed dancing, hunting, feasting, and all the other things that people of the time enjoyed. Other people say that fairy tales began as stories of gods and goddesses who were worshipped in ancient times.

One thing is certain: The fairies of the stories were no ordinary mortals. They were said to live long—many, many times as long as the oldest person. Fairy time was not at all the same as human time. One Irish tale tells of a young boy who wandered into the forest and heard the sound of beautiful singing. Enchanted, he leaned up against a tree to listen for a while. When he returned to his house, he found that his family had been dead for many years—a hundred years of human time had been just a few hours to the fairies.

Fairies could take the shapes of rocks, trees, or animals. They could appear and disappear at will. And, most of the time, they chose to be invisible to humans. A traveler once rounded a bend in the road and beheld a beautiful sight: a fairy market, with gaily colored tents and crowds of beautiful fairies around them. When he ran to the place, everything disappeared—but he knew his eyes hadn't deceived him because he could feel the pushing and shoving of the crowd!

The tall fairies of old tales had great magic powers, and it was dangerous to have dealings with them. One story tells of a village woman who was called to assist at the birth of a fairy baby. The fairies gave her some ointment to rub on the baby, and by accident she got some in her eye. After that, much to her surprise, she found that she could see the fairies anytime. But one day, when she greeted a passing fairy, he stopped and asked her which eye she saw him through. When she answered, he struck that eye and blinded it—so that she would never see fairies again.

The story of Sleeping Beauty (which has many different versions) shows the risks of insulting a fairy. In this tale, a king wanted to invite the fairies who lived in his realm to his baby daughter's christening. One fairy, however, wasn't invited. She was furious at having been left out, and appeared at the feast and laid a curse on the child—that she would prick her finger on a spindle at the age of 16 and die. One of the other fairies managed to soften the curse: The princess wouldn't die, but would sleep for a hundred years.

Other stories tell that fairies sometimes kidnapped people and held them captive in their magic kingdoms. And sometimes they stole human babies, putting a fairy baby in the crib instead. The parents would have to do something extraordinary to get this changeling, as the fairy baby was called, to reveal itself. It was said, for example, that if you brewed ale in an eggshell, the changeling would exclaim in surprise.

But fairies were by no means always evil. Some farmers believed that the fairies would bless their crops and ensure a good harvest. In a tale from Scotland, a young man was changed into a lizard by a witch. He lay by a tree, trapped in his ugly body, until a troop of fairies passed by. Their queen took pity on him and restored him to his human form.

In an Irish story, a chieftain named Teigue was sailing in pursuit of an enemy when a storm blew him across the invisible boundary between the real world and the fairy world. He landed on a fairy island, where the queen welcomed him warmly. She sent him on his way with a magic emerald cup that would protect him from harm, and a flock of enchanted birds that would guide him.

23

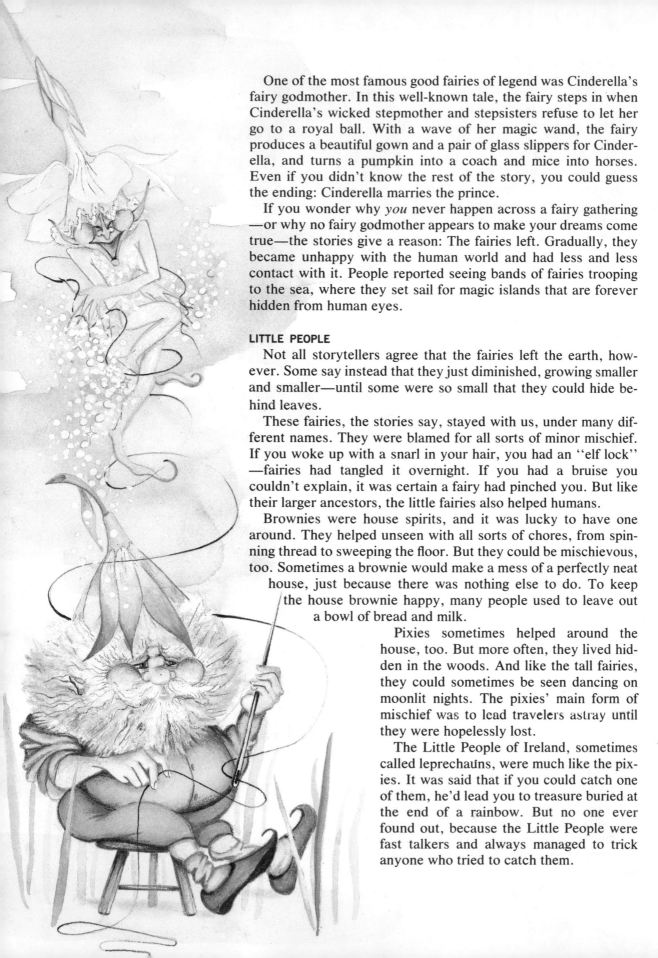

One of the most famous good fairies of legend was Cinderella's fairy godmother. In this well-known tale, the fairy steps in when Cinderella's wicked stepmother and stepsisters refuse to let her go to a royal ball. With a wave of her magic wand, the fairy produces a beautiful gown and a pair of glass slippers for Cinderella, and turns a pumpkin into a coach and mice into horses. Even if you didn't know the rest of the story, you could guess the ending: Cinderella marries the prince.

If you wonder why *you* never happen across a fairy gathering —or why no fairy godmother appears to make your dreams come true—the stories give a reason: The fairies left. Gradually, they became unhappy with the human world and had less and less contact with it. People reported seeing bands of fairies trooping to the sea, where they set sail for magic islands that are forever hidden from human eyes.

LITTLE PEOPLE

Not all storytellers agree that the fairies left the earth, however. Some say instead that they just diminished, growing smaller and smaller—until some were so small that they could hide behind leaves.

These fairies, the stories say, stayed with us, under many different names. They were blamed for all sorts of minor mischief. If you woke up with a snarl in your hair, you had an "elf lock" —fairies had tangled it overnight. If you had a bruise you couldn't explain, it was certain a fairy had pinched you. But like their larger ancestors, the little fairies also helped humans.

Brownies were house spirits, and it was lucky to have one around. They helped unseen with all sorts of chores, from spinning thread to sweeping the floor. But they could be mischievous, too. Sometimes a brownie would make a mess of a perfectly neat house, just because there was nothing else to do. To keep the house brownie happy, many people used to leave out a bowl of bread and milk.

Pixies sometimes helped around the house, too. But more often, they lived hidden in the woods. And like the tall fairies, they could sometimes be seen dancing on moonlit nights. The pixies' main form of mischief was to lead travelers astray until they were hopelessly lost.

The Little People of Ireland, sometimes called leprechauns, were much like the pixies. It was said that if you could catch one of them, he'd lead you to treasure buried at the end of a rainbow. But no one ever found out, because the Little People were fast talkers and always managed to trick anyone who tried to catch them.

Some Swedish elves began as tall fairies, but in later tales they were the smallest of the little fairies—less than a foot high, with gauzy wings. They were gentle nature spirits who could sit on flowers and talk to the birds, and it was thought that they helped flowers bloom and the seasons change.

Other stories depict elves as more like pixies and brownies. In the story of the shoemaker and the elves, for example, an old shoemaker finds that tiny elves are coming to his shop every night and doing his work for him. Delighted, he and his wife decide to reward the elves by making new suits of clothes for them. Unfortunately, the elves are so pleased with the new clothes that they put them on immediately and dance out the door, never to be seen again.

Do such creatures really exist? In 1917, two young girls in Cottingley, England, claimed to have seen a band of little fairies —and even to have danced with them. To prove their story, they borrowed a camera and took pictures of the little people. The pictures of the Cottingley Fairies caused quite a stir, and at the time many people thought they were genuine. Modern researchers, however, say that the pictures were faked.

So there is still no evidence that fairies exist, or that they ever did. But that hasn't stopped people from enjoying stories about them—or from making up new ones. Tinker Bell, in the story of Peter Pan, may be the best-known fairy of modern times. She is a tiny winged creature who can do both magic and mischief, and like many other fairies she's quick to take offense.

Modern authors have also drawn on some of the older fairy legends. J. R. R. Tolkien, in his book *The Hobbit* and his trilogy *The Lord of the Rings,* created a fantasy world where humans live side by side with all sorts of strange creatures. The elves in these books are very like the tall and beautiful fairies of old. And like them, they leave the earth, sailing west to a land where mortals cannot go.

Proof or no proof, the next time you see the leaves flutter, you just might want to take a closer look!

SLOTHS: JUST HANGIN' AROUND

Even its name is an insult—sloth, a synonym for laziness. The sleepy, slow-moving sloth has been called moronic, wretched, an "imperfect sketch" drawn by nature, even a "defective monster."

In fact, the sloth has been much misunderstood. Scientists are learning that these mammals are actually perfectly tailored to their environment. Sloths live in the treetop canopies of the tropical rain forests in South and Central America. They survive on a low-energy diet made up mostly of leaves. Since the sloth takes in so little energy in its food, it also expends very little energy—and its body and habits are perfectly designed to save effort.

One of nature's slowest creatures, the sloth spends its life just hanging around. Specifically, it hangs upside down on the branches of trees in the rain forests. With their long, hooklike claws, sloths can cling so tightly to the branches that sometimes the only way to capture one is to cut off the branch it's gripping.

TWO TOES OR THREE

There are two types of sloths: the two-toed sloth (with two claws on its front paws) and the three-toed sloth (with three claws in front). They are the last survivors of an animal family that once included giant ground sloths, some of which were as big as elephants. Ground sloths died out about 10,000 years ago. The two modern sloth types differ from each other in many ways, and there are several species of each type. But all have become specially adapted to life in the green and leafy world of the treetops.

All sloths have thick, shaggy fur; long limbs (longer in front than behind); short, stubby tails; and flat faces with short snouts and tiny ears. The shape of a three-toed sloth's muzzle gives the impression that the animal is always smiling, even when it's asleep. These sloths also have dark markings around their eyes, to fool predators into thinking they're awake when they're not.

The sloth's body structure helps it save energy. Its weight is low—about 20 pounds

(9 kilograms) for a two-toed sloth, half that for a three-toed sloth. And sloths have very little muscle, only half the amount that most similar-sized mammals have. Maintaining muscle tissue requires a lot of energy—and, after all, you only need muscles if you're going to move around.

Two-toed sloths are slightly more active than three-toed sloths. They have sharp canine teeth and will bite or lash out with their claws if they are disturbed. A three-toed sloth will just cling tighter to its branch; it can't bite because it has no front teeth. Some don't move even when a gun is fired at close range. In any case, sloths are nearsighted and don't see very far. They're also somewhat hard of hearing, but their sense of taste is good.

Sloths are the most numerous mammals in the rain forest; there are many more sloths than monkeys. But visitors to the forest rarely notice the sloths because they move so little and are usually silent. Three-toed sloths have a distinctive cry of distress—"ay-ee"—which has led Brazilians to name them ais. But the cry of distress isn't often heard.

Sloths are so lethargic and unaware of their surroundings that you'd expect them to be easy marks for predators. But in fact, many sloths survive to enjoy a peaceful old age. Not only are they hard for predators to spot, they're also well protected with shaggy fur, thick skin, and extra ribs. They may live as long as 30 or 40 years—and all that time, they do as little as possible.

A SLOTHFUL LIFE

Most of the time—up to twenty hours a day—the sloth is asleep, curled up in the crotch of a tree or hanging from a branch. When it tucks in its head and its short, rounded tail to doze off, a sloth looks like what one scientist called a "hanging animal basket." It also looks something like a wasps' nest, so predators tend to pass by. Predators also ignore the sloth because it blends in with the background of branches and leaves. The sloth's fur is naturally brownish gray. But each hair is scored with tiny grooves, where algae grow. Thus the sloth's coat has a greenish tinge.

The coat is unusual in another way: It's parted along the animal's stomach, instead of along its back (as is the case with most other mammals). This means that the coat sheds rainwater well when the sloth is hanging upside down, so there's no need to run for cover in the rain forest's frequent showers. The thick fur also acts as an excellent insulator—so the sloth doesn't have to waste energy keeping its body temperature up.

Even with their fur coats, sloths don't maintain a constant body temperature the way most mammals do. To save energy, their body temperature drops when they're asleep. Three-toed sloths climb (slowly) to the tops of their trees to warm themselves in the sunlight when they awake. Two-toed sloths are nocturnal (active at night). Being a bit more lively by nature, they can warm themselves by moving around.

When the sloth isn't sleeping, it's doing next to nothing—munching a few leaves, perhaps, or moving (ever so slowly) from branch to branch. The animal's curved claws, long arms, and flexible joints ensure

that it doesn't have to move too much to get a meal. It just reaches out in a leisurely fashion to grab a leaf. Its head can rotate as much as 270 degrees on its neck, so it doesn't have to move its body to look around. Three-toed sloths have extra vertebrae in their necks, making it even easier to reach nearby leaves. The sloth tears off a bit of leaf with its leathery lips and (slowly) chews it with its peglike back teeth.

Two-toed sloths can get along on just about any leafy diet, and they eat fruit and flowers as well. They may also raid birds' nests for eggs. But three-toed sloths have more finicky eating habits. Scientists think that each three-toed sloth learns from its mother to eat the leaves of only certain types of trees. Since different sloths learn different feeding patterns, many can live in the forest together without competing against each other for food. But three-toed sloths are almost impossible to keep in captivity because each requires an individual diet. The sloths you see in zoos are two-toed sloths.

Just as the sloth eats slowly, it digests slowly. A sloth's stomach is usually full because the supply of leaves in the rain forest is ample. The stomach is so large that, together with its contents, it may make up more than a fourth of the animal's weight. Bacteria in the stomach help digest the leaves, but the process is measured in days. Three-toed sloths eliminate about once every eight days; two-toed sloths, only slightly more often. Both types laboriously climb down to the bases of their trees to deposit their dung and then slowly climb up again.

As you might expect, sloths don't put a great deal of effort into grooming themselves. A sloth's coat is, often, a mess. It's also home to many other creatures—hundreds of beetles, ticks, and mites, as well as moths that lay their eggs in the fur. When the moth larvae hatch, they feed on the algae growing there.

Sloths are rarely seen on the ground—and with good reason. Some two-toed sloths can

The slow-moving sloth survives on a low-energy diet made up mostly of leaves.

A newborn sloth clings to its mother's fur until it's six to nine months old.

walk awkwardly on the ground, but three-toed sloths have so little muscle that they can't even stand on all fours. They must crawl, reaching out with their front claws to grasp something and then dragging their bodies up to it. For this reason, most sloths use the branches to move from tree to tree: The sloth crawls out to the tip of a branch and waits for a gust of wind to blow a branch from a neighboring tree within its reach. Then it grasps the new branch and lets itself be pulled into the new tree.

Sloths are excellent swimmers, however. Their fur traps air, and this, combined with their light weight and large stomachs, helps them bob along like floats when they must cross forest streams.

A SLOTH FAMILY

In the wild, sloths live alone. Baby sloths are born singly, usually once a year. Often the birth takes place as the mother is dangling from a tree branch. The newborn sloth clings to the fur of its mother's chest and stays hidden, nursing, for the first few weeks of life. Then it begins to reach out and grab leaves to sniff them, and also to nibble some

of the mother's food. The female raises her baby on her own; the male takes no part in the family.

A baby sloth is a little acrobat, with many times more energy than its parents. It has to be, because its mother takes no notice of it as she climbs about the trees. If the young sloth doesn't pay attention, it may be squeezed or scraped off by a passing branch. So it nimbly hops off, scampers around the obstacle, and jumps back on its mother on the other side. At the rate adult sloths move, there's plenty of time.

The young sloth continues to cling to its mother's fur until it's six to nine months old. During this time it learns which leaves are edible and which trees should be avoided. Then the mother leaves, and the young sloth is on its own in its familiar territory. Six months later, the mother returns, often with a new baby. Then the young sloth must move off to find a territory of its own.

Sloths are full-grown when they're about 6 years old. By that time, they've acquired all the laziness of their parents. They're ready for a long and drowsy life of doing nothing—slowly.

A DELICATE ART

Lush flowers, an ancient emperor, a watchful cat—these are examples of one of the most beautiful and delicate folk crafts: Chinese paper cutting.

Scissors or sharp knives are used to cut the paper. The artist doesn't sketch or mark the paper in advance but simply starts cutting, carefully moving the scissors until the cut lines have formed a flower, an animal, or a human being. The artist may then paint the designs.

This craft is centuries old and is popular among people of all ages and all walks of life. The Chinese use papercuts to decorate their homes or as stencil designs for fabrics and ceramics.

31

The greedy trolls

Once upon a time there was a pleasant, sunny, and peaceful valley, with a great, big tree in the middle of it. People came from miles around to picnic and play with their friends there.

The big tree was home to all sorts of birds, squirrels, and chipmunks. If you wanted to, you could lie down in the tall grass and take a nap, or look up at the clouds and imagine that they were white, puffy animals floating overhead.

It was a cozy place to be. That's why Jonathan and his sister, Miriam, loved to go there whenever they could.

Jonathan loved to climb in the tree with the other boys, and Miriam loved to play hide-and-seek with the other girls. Sometimes all the boys and girls together would play a great big game of tag around the tree.

One day a family of trolls came to the valley. They tramped right through the children's favorite picnic spot and stopped at the big tree.

"This looks like a good place to dig a home," grunted the papa troll.

"Oh, yes!" said the mama troll. "It's much too nice to leave it alone."

"I bet picnickers come here," exclaimed the little boy troll.

"We'll be able to take their picnic food," said the little girl troll.

"Yes, I think we're going to like it here very much," snarled the papa troll.

The troll family started digging their home under the roots of the big tree. They dug day and night for a week, piling dirt everywhere. And it wasn't long before the big tree started to die.

"Ah! This is perfect," chortled the papa troll. "There's nothing better than a dark, musty home under the roots of a dying tree."

When they had finished digging, the trolls settled down to wait for the picnickers.

The next day Jonathan and Miriam came to the valley for a picnic. They set their picnic blanket and basket out near the big tree. Suddenly, the trolls popped out from under the roots of the big tree and grabbed all their picnic food.

"Oh, boy!" giggled the little boy and girl troll. "Apples, peaches, cherries, strawberries, blueberries, chestnuts, hickory nuts, and walnuts!"

"Hey! Why did you take all our picnic food?" yelled Jonathan.

"Because taking things is what trolls do best," laughed the little boy troll. Then he disappeared under the tree.

"We work for the ogre in the next valley," snarled the papa troll. "He's going to pay us for coming to valleys like this and taking things."

Then the entire troll family scurried back into their home under the roots of the big tree.

"Well, I guess next time we'd better picnic in the middle of an open field," said Miriam, slamming the lid shut on their empty picnic basket.

The next day, Jonathan and Miriam spread their picnic blanket out in the middle of an open field, far away from the big tree. But the trolls only burrowed under the ground, popped up next to the picnic blanket, and grabbed everything they could.

"Next time we come here, we'll just have to leave all our food at home," complained Miriam.

"Yeah. Otherwise the trolls will just take it," added Jonathan.

The next day Jonathan and Miriam spread their picnic blanket out in the middle of another open field and, sure enough, the trolls popped up from under the ground to grab all the picnic food. They were surprised to learn there was nothing to grab.

"Silly trolls!" laughed Miriam. "How does it feel to have nothing to grab?"

Jonathan and Miriam picked up their picnic blanket and ran home, laughing all the way.

"Well, if that's the way it's going to be," snorted the papa troll, "we'll just have to find something else to take. Our boss, the ogre, will be coming soon, and we've got to show him we're doing a good job."

So the trolls began taking all the fruit from the trees in the valley and stashing it in their

dark home under the roots of the big tree. Then they took all the berries from the berry bushes in the valley. And then they took all the nuts from all the nut trees. They even took the eggs from the birds' nests.

And when the trolls had taken everything, the birds, squirrels, and chipmunks moved away from the valley, because there was nothing left to eat.

The troll family sat in their dark and dingy home under the roots of the big tree for three days, waiting for the ogre to arrive.

"Papa, the nuts are getting stale, the berries are drying out, and the fruit is starting to rot," said the little boy troll.

"Maybe so," answered the papa troll, "but at least we've got it all!"

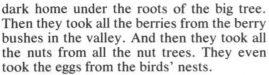

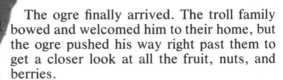

The ogre finally arrived. The troll family bowed and welcomed him to their home, but the ogre pushed his way right past them to get a closer look at all the fruit, nuts, and berries.

"Give me that and that and those and that and these and this and that and those!" he snorted as he grabbed everything he could, which was everything the trolls had.

The ogre dragged everything out of the trolls' home. Stopping in front of the hole in the ground that served as a front door, he threw each of the trolls a rotten peach and said, "You're all fired!"

The trolls watched in disbelief as the ogre disappeared from view.

"Well, how do you like that?" grumbled the papa troll.

"He didn't even give us two weeks' notice," said the mama troll.

"These peaches he left us are too rotten to eat," complained the little boy troll.

"I'm hungry!" cried the little girl troll.

Squatting at the base of the big tree, the trolls all started crying and wailing.

Jonathan and Miriam heard the crying and wailing and came to the valley to see what it was all about. They brought a picnic basket full of food with them, just in case.

From a nearby hill overlooking the big tree, Jonathan and Miriam could see the troll family. As soon as they set out their picnic blanket and basket, the trolls spotted them.

"Uh-oh, here they come again," sighed Miriam.

But this time the trolls didn't take anything. Instead, they just sat around Jonathan and Miriam and watched them picnic.

"Let's offer them something from our picnic basket," said Miriam.

Jonathan reached into the basket and pulled out a nice, ripe peach. He handed it to the mama troll. The mama troll accepted the peach, but she didn't eat it. Instead, she gave it to the little boy troll.

The little boy troll passed the peach to the little girl troll. "You're the one who's hungry," he said.

"Thank you," she said, taking a bite out of the juicy peach.

Jonathan and Miriam passed out more food, including apples and cherries, and nuts and berries, so that everyone in the troll family had something.

"This is fun! I'd much rather give food to you trolls than have you take it from me," observed Miriam.

"We'd rather have people give us food than take it, too," admitted the papa troll. "I really didn't like the job in the first place."

"The pay was lousy, too," snorted the mama troll.

"Well," said Jonathan, "this is a better way to make friends, I think."

Soon the fruit, nuts, and berries were growing on the trees again. Then all the birds, squirrels, and chipmunks came back to the valley.

It was no time at all before Jonathan and Miriam and all their friends were playing and picnicking with the troll family.

The trolls were especially good at playing hide-and-seek.

CUTE CATERPILLARS

Liven up your room with CUTE CATERPILLARS! These crazy,
creepy critters can be made from kneesocks or from a com-
bination of anklesocks and leg warmers. Wildly patterned
ones work best. First make the caterpillar's head by stuffing
the toe of a sock with fiberfill or some other material. Tie
off the head with a colorful ponytail elastic or piece of yarn.

Then stuff the next section and tie it off. Keep going until you reach the end of the sock. Now add the details. Try brightly colored pipe-cleaner antennas. Glue on plastic eyes or make eyes and other parts out of felt. How about a glittering rhinestone nose? Give the caterpillar false eyelashes, pipe-cleaner legs, and a giant pompom tail. Be creative.

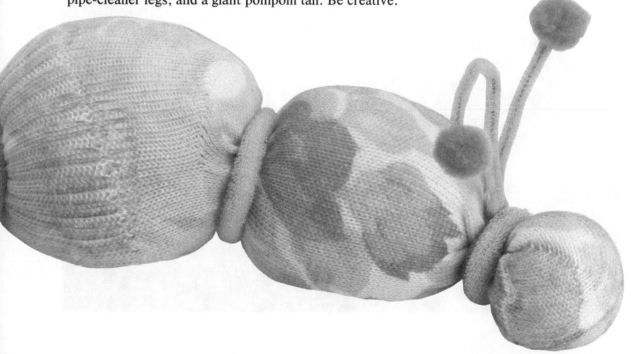

NATURE'S VANISHING RAIN FORESTS

Enter the dim, green world of the tropical rain forest. As you walk down the forest trail, huge trees surround you. Tropical vines hang from their limbs, and far above you their leafy branches form a rooflike canopy that blocks out the sun. The air is warm, damp, and heavy.

High above, you hear the calls of howler monkeys and parrots and other exotic birds. But on the forest floor, you see few signs of life. Every so often you hear a soft rustle as a toad or some other small creature hops away, startled by your footsteps. And now and then you spot a brilliant blue butterfly, fluttering through the dim light. Be careful to stay on the trail—the tree trunks look so much alike that it's easy to get lost. And keep your eyes open for snakes.

Tropical rain forests like the one you have entered cover a narrow band of the Earth near the equator. They are found in Africa, South and Central America, Asia, and Oceania. (The world's largest rain forest is around the Amazon River, in Brazil.) They get their name from the fact that it rains there almost every day—which also accounts for the heavy, damp air. And, although you may see few animals as you walk along the forest floor, rain forests actually teem with life. More than a third of the world's animal and plant species live there, and scientists believe that the tropical habitat is home to many others that haven't even been discovered yet.

But the rain forests are disappearing at an alarming rate: More than 50 acres (20 hectares) of forest are cut every minute, as people take the trees for lumber and the land for farms, roads, and other types of development. Thus scientists are rushing to study these exotic living laboratories before they vanish. And conservationists are working on plans to save as much of the rain forests as they can.

THE RAIN FOREST FLOOR

Tropical rain forests are one of the world's last great wilderness areas. Few people live in them, and many regions of the forests have never been explored. The forests took centuries to develop—some of the tropical trees that now tower hundreds of feet above the ground were saplings when Columbus sailed to the New World. Unlike northern forests, where you will see many trees of the same species grouped together in clumps and stands, the tropical rain forest contains a seemingly endless variety of different types of trees.

The dense shade cast by the canopy of the treetops means that there is no tangle of underbrush on the forest floor—without sunlight, plants can't grow. Instead, just a few species of ferns and similar plants survive in the open spaces between the tree trunks. Some trees have huge "buttress" roots that flare out from the trunks 20 feet (6 meters) above the ground. The roots extend down into the soil, and scientists think they help anchor the trees in the thin leaf mold that carpets the forest floor.

The soil of the floor isn't rich, and some trees and plants have developed other ways of getting the nutrients they need. For example, special types of fungi grow around the tree roots and help the trees break down the few nutrients that the soil does contain. And some trees have developed above-ground roots that trap water and minerals in the air. The soil is so poor, in fact, that when land has been cleared for farming, people often find that it will support crops for only a year or two.

Sometimes there's a break in the canopy —because a tree has fallen, or because a stream has cut its way through the forest. Then sunlight can enter, and the forest produces a riot of vines, shrubs, and flowering plants. Animals congregate in these spots, too—monkeys, iridescent butterflies, and brightly colored birds such as parrots, toucans, and orioles. In the South American forests, there are brilliant red and blue arrow poison frogs, whose bright colors warn predators of the deadly poison they secrete on their skins. And always, there are snakes that hang like vines from tree limbs.

Forest streams also teem with life. In many places, there are strange species of fish. In the forests around the Amazon, for

Most of the life of the tropical rain forest is found far above the ground, in the treetop canopy. There, huge leafy branches spread horizontally, forming a dense "forest above the forest." And that layer supports an almost endless variety of plants and animals.

Marmoset

Torch ginger flower

Quetzal

Heliconia

Variegated squirrel

Harlequin beetle

example, one type of fish has flat-topped teeth like those found in cows and other grazing animals. The teeth have a purpose—for two to four months a year, when the Amazon's waters are high, the river spills over its banks and floods the forest floor. Then the fish can swim out through the forest and eat the seeds, fruit, and nuts that they find there. Other fish have the remarkable ability to breathe air during the brief dry seasons when forest ponds shrink. They do this through a special collection of blood vessels in their foreheads. These vessels work much like human lungs, pumping oxygen directly into the bloodstream.

One reason you see so few signs of life as you walk through the forest is that many of the animals are nocturnal—they sleep during the day and come out to hunt for food at night. But the biggest reason is that most of the life of the forest is found far above the ground, in the treetop canopy.

STUDYING THE CANOPY

Scientists are racing against time to study the rain-forest canopies before they are destroyed. But they face special risks and problems in their work. The first problem is getting up to the treetops.

Climbing the trees isn't a good solution—snakes and scorpions lie in wait along the branches. Some researchers build towers up to treetop level. Others use "cherrypickers"—the mechanical lifts often used in tree work and fruit harvesting. One scientist studying the rain forest in Costa Rica climbs into the trees on ropes and constructs a platform in the branches. Then he assembles a network of ropes, like a spider web, that allows him to move from tree to tree.

The dangers don't end when the researchers are in the trees. Violent storms can uproot the trees, and there's always the risk of a fall. Still, dedicated researchers continue to climb into the canopy, to see first-hand one of the least-studied habitats on Earth.

THE TREETOP CANOPY

The rain-forest canopy is a completely different world. Here, in the sunlight 50 to 200 feet (15 to 60 meters) above the ground, the huge trees send out massive horizontal branches. And they support an almost endless variety of life forms—from birds, bats, and butterflies to mice, monkeys, and countless other, more exotic animals. Many of the creatures that live here spend their entire lives in the treetops, rarely or never setting foot on the ground.

The key to life high above the ground is interdependence: The plants and animals of the canopy depend on each other to stay alive. For example, a strange plant called the trashbasket plant anchors itself to tree limbs. It traps debris that falls from higher in the canopy and turns this material into nutrient-rich humus. The humus supports not only the plant but also insects like earthworms and centipedes.

Many other plants grow in the treetops, too. Most of these are epiphytes—plants that grow on tree limbs and take the moisture and nutrients they need from the air rather than from the soil. There are countless epiphytic varieties of orchids, mosses, lichens, and ferns. One epiphyte, a spiky-topped plant called the bromeliad, helps nurture baby frogs. The leaves of this plant trap water, and tree frogs place their eggs there. When the eggs hatch, the tadpoles can swim about in the water caught by the plant.

A few of the mightiest trees depend on single species of insects to reproduce. The flower of the Brazil nut, for example, is so tightly closed that only one bee, the carpenter bee, is able to open it. Without this bee, the flowers couldn't be pollinated, and no seeds would be produced. The many species of tropical fig trees in the rain forest depend on tiny fig wasps for pollination. The wasps in turn lay their eggs in the tree's fruit.

Some species of insects also depend on each other. In South America, for example, wasps bore holes in the long hanging nests of Azteca ants. The Azteca ants then protect the wasps from their main predators, the army ants. And the stinging wasps in turn protect the Azteca ants from anteaters that climb into the trees in search of food.

Sometimes the chain of interdependence extends back down to the forest floor. Several species of birds, for example, follow army ants as they march across the floor looking for food. The birds eat insects that the army ants flush out, and they in turn are followed by butterflies that feed on their droppings.

One of the best-known treetop dwellers is the sloth—a mammal that hangs upside-down from the tree limbs and sleeps most of the time. More than twenty species of insects, including several moths and beetles, live in the sloth's furry coat. A type of algae also grows on the coat, giving the animal a greenish tint that helps it stay camouflaged among the leaves.

Like other tree-living animals, the sloth is specially adapted to its home: It has long limbs and grasping hands that help it reach and hold vines and tree branches, and its eyes are positioned looking forward, for good depth perception. The many species of monkeys that live in the canopy also have these traits. Treetop animals seem to share still another trait—intelligence. Parrots, which are said to be among the smartest of birds, live in the rain-forest canopy. And the coati, a raccoonlike animal that also lives in the treetops, uses basic reasoning to get its food, much as a chimpanzee does.

THE FUTURE OF THE RAIN FORESTS

It seems likely that as more acres of forest are cut, many of the rain forest plants and animals will become extinct. This is because so many of these plants and animals depend closely on each other. Yet the outlook for saving the forests isn't good. Most of the forests are in developing countries that badly need both farmland and the income from lumber that cutting the forests provides.

But there are ways in which the uncut forests can provide income. Brazil nuts already are an important crop in South America. And some countries have started to experiment with other ways of producing crops from the rain forest—oil from oil palms, for example, and certain fast-growing trees that can be raised and harvested for lumber. Other tropical plants provide valuable chemicals that can be used in medicines and insecticides, and they might be grown for those purposes. With careful planning and good conservation, the tropical rain forests may yet be saved.

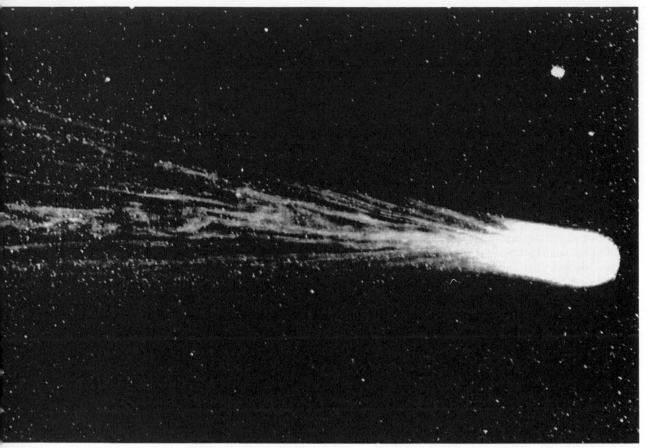

Halley's comet—a special visitor from outer space that won't be seen again until the year 2061.

THE RETURN OF HALLEY'S COMET

In 1986, a very special visitor from outer space returned—Halley's comet. People had waited 76 years for the event. The comet's last visit had occurred in 1910. "It was scary then . . . like a blowtorch in the sky," said an elderly man who remembered that visit.

"This is a poor excuse for what it was in 1910," the man said when he saw the comet in 1986. Indeed, the view of the comet from Earth was nowhere near as brilliant as in the previous encounter. This was largely due to the fact that Earth was a month further back on its orbit than it had been in 1910. So instead of coming within 14,000,000 miles (23,000,000 kilometers) of Halley's comet, as we had in 1910, our closest encounter was 39,000,000 miles (63,000,000 kilometers).

Despite the disappointment felt by some people, the 1986 visit was a huge success as far as scientists were concerned. More than 1,000 astronomers participated in International Halley Watch, using the world's most powerful telescopes to track the comet. They also had an array of sophisticated instruments aboard five unmanned spacecraft that had been launched especially to obtain data on the comet.

Two of the spacecraft, Suisei and Saki-gake, were launched by Japan. Their primary objective was to study the interaction of the comet with the solar wind. (The solar wind is a stream of charged particles—mostly protons and electrons—that flow away from the sun.)

Two more craft, Vega 1 and Vega 2, were launched by the Soviet Union. They carried cameras and various instruments, including dust collectors provided by American scientists. In early March, these craft flew within 5,300 miles (8,500 kilometers) of the comet and returned many excellent photographs and other data.

The closest approach to Halley's comet was made by the European Space Agency's craft Giotto. (This vehicle was named after the 14th-century Florentine painter Giotto di Bondone. It is believed that he used a 1301 sighting of Halley's comet as the model for the Star of Bethlehem in his famous nativity scene, *Adoration of the Magi*.) On March 14, Giotto flew within 335 miles (540 kilometers) of the comet's nucleus. Its television cameras and instruments provided extremely detailed information about the nucleus.

As a result of all these investigations, more was learned about comets in 1986 than had been learned in all the centuries before.

A GIANT EXCLAMATION POINT!

Halley's comet travels in an elliptical orbit that is more than 7 billion miles (11 billion kilometers) long. During most of its travels it consists only of a small, solid, icy nucleus. But as the comet approaches the sun, solar radiation causes the nucleus' ice particles to vaporize and form gases. These gases, together with some dust that escapes from the nucleus, form a fuzzy cloud, called the coma, around the nucleus. This glowing coma makes it impossible to see the actual nucleus from Earth.

The long tail is formed by the solar wind, which pushes some of the coma material away from the sun. A comet's tail is always

A color-enhanced photo (which helps to show details) of the comet's coma and nucleus. The nucleus is the dark mass at the upper left. Space probe photos showed that the nucleus was "the darkest dark" imaginable.

Dr. Halley.

HOW THE COMET GOT ITS NAME

Most comets are named after their discoverers. But Halley's comet had been seen by people long before it was named after Edmund Halley (his name rhymes with "alley").

Edmund Halley was an English astronomer who lived from 1656 to 1742. At that time, the people believed that each comet was on a one-way trip—that it streaked through the solar system only once, never to be seen again. But Halley believed that comets traveled in orbits that would periodically bring them back to Earth's vicinity. And he believed that the comet he had seen in 1682 was the same one that people had seen in 1531 and 1607. In his book *Synopsis astronomiae cometicae,* Halley predicted that this comet would return again in or about the year 1758.

On Christmas night, 1758, sixteen years after Halley's death, a German farmer and amateur astronomer studied the sky through his telescope and became the first person to witness the return of the comet that year. Halley's prediction that comets travel in orbits around the sun was confirmed. And the comet has carried his name ever since.

on the side *away* from the sun. It's behind the nucleus as the comet races toward the sun—and ahead of the nucleus as the comet streaks past the sun.

The nearer a comet gets to the sun, the brighter and longer its tail becomes. Soon the comet looks like a giant exclamation point in the sky. (Comets, like planets, don't emit light. Rather, they are visible primarily because they reflect sunlight.)

The tail may be tens of millions of miles long and easily visible through telescopes. But it contains very little material. It is a better vacuum than any vacuum scientists can create on Earth. In fact, if all the matter in a comet's tail could be gathered together, it would easily fit into your home.

A BLACK SNOWBALL

Before 1986, the composition of comets was unknown. The most widely accepted theory, proposed in 1950 by astronomer Fred L. Whipple, suggested that a comet's nucleus resembled a dirty snowball. This "snowball" was thought to be a mass of frozen matter, consisting of ice, carbon dioxide and other frozen gases, and small particles of dust and minerals. Data collected by Giotto and the Vegas confirmed Whipple's theory, but with some unexpected twists.

First, Halley's nucleus was bigger than expected. It measured 10 miles (16 kilometers) long and 5 miles (7.5 kilometers) wide. And it wasn't a round ball. Instead, it was shaped like a peanut or a lumpy potato.

The surface of the nucleus was uneven, with ridges and valleys. And it was black—"very dark, the darkest dark you can imagine," said a European Space Agency scientist. This black coating acts as an insulator. It keeps the surface of the nucleus warm despite the underlying ice. An infrared scanner on Vega 1 found that surface temperatures in one region of the nucleus were about 85°F (28°C).

More than 80 percent of the gas blowing out from the nucleus, as it neared the sun, was water vapor. And there was a lot of it: The sun's heat caused the nucleus to lose at least 40 tons a second! Furthermore, it appeared that this evaporation was occurring only from certain parts of the nucleus: Photographs taken by Giotto showed narrow jets of gas and dust coming from six or seven vents, and all the vents were on the side of the nucleus facing the sun.

Every time Halley's comet nears the sun, part of its nucleus evaporates. Eventually, the comet will disintegrate completely. This has happened to many other comets. But it won't happen to Halley's comet for a long time. Scientists expect this comet to continue on its orbit for hundreds of thousands, perhaps millions, of years.

A HISTORY OF FEAR AND SUPERSTITION

Halley's comet has been known to people for thousands of years. Chinese astronomers were believed to have sighted it in 240 B.C. The Babylonians recorded its appearances in 164 B.C. and in 87 B.C.

In those long ago times, people had little knowledge of astronomy. Many myths arose to explain these objects that blazed across the night skies. The Chinese thought comets were "broom stars," used by the gods to sweep evil out of the heavens. The evil then fell to Earth, bringing disasters.

People elsewhere also believed that comets foretold terrible events. In A.D. 66, Halley's comet was said to hang like "the blade of a sword" over Jerusalem. Historians viewed this as a warning that told of the city's fall to the Romans four years later. The 1066 appearance of the comet was blamed for the Norman conquest of England. And its 1456 appearance was associated with the fall of Constantinople to the Turks and future Turkish victories. The victors in these battles, however, may have viewed the comet's appearance in a more positive light!

Edmund Halley's discovery that comets travel in orbits and don't just "appear" helped dispel many of the superstitions about comets. But some people continued to fear them. In 1910, after astronomers announced that Earth would pass through the tail of Halley's comet, thousands of people panicked. Fearing they would die from poisonous gases in the tail, they bought "comet pills" and gas masks. In many places, people refused to work, children asked teachers for permission to stay home from school, and priests and ministers were besieged by calls asking for reassurance.

The year 1986 marked the 30th recorded passage of Halley's comet. There was no fear, but lots of fuss. People took out their telescopes and binoculars to try to get a glimpse of the comet. They signed up for trips to the Australian outback and other exotic viewing places. They bought commemorative stamps, T-shirts, gym bags, posters, pins, and other trinkets.

For many people, the views were disappointing. But perhaps more spectacular views will occur in 2061, when Halley is scheduled to make its next visit. So mark your calendar!

JENNY TESAR
Designer, Computer Programs

47

HATS OFF!

People wear all sorts of hats for all sorts of occasions. There are work hats and party hats. There are hats for special events, such as the mortarboards worn by graduating students. There are even hats, such as nightcaps, that you wouldn't want your best friend to see you wearing!

Through the ages, fashions in headwear have changed often. Some styles that were once very popular are no longer seen. For instance, in medieval Europe wealthy women often wore tall, pointed hats called hennins. The hats looked a bit like ice-cream cones, and some reached incredible heights.

The hennin and seventeen other types of hats are illustrated below. Match the illustrations with the names in the list on the right. If some of the hats are unfamiliar to you, look in your dictionary for descriptions of them.

1. boater
2. beret
3. bonnet
4. bowler (or derby)
5. cloche
6. coolie
7. deerstalker
8. fez
9. hennin
10. miter
11. mortarboard
12. nightcap
13. sombrero
14. ten-gallon
15. top hat
16. tricorn
17. turban
18. tyrolean

ANSWERS: 1,p; 2,m; 3,r; 4,i; 5,n; 6,l; 7,k; 8,h; 9,b; 10,d; 11,q; 12,c; 13,a; 14,o; 15,f; 16,g; 17,j; 18,e.

Next, go on a word hunt. Hidden in this search-a-word puzzle are the names of all eighteen hats. Try to find them. Cover the puzzle with a sheet of tracing paper. Read forward, backward, up, down, and diagonally. Then shade in the letters of each hat as you find it. One hat has been shaded in for you.

D	R	A	O	B	R	A	T	R	O	M	N	C
I	E	H	E	N	N	I	N	O	G	L	O	H
N	I	E	L	I	V	A	M	P	P	O	L	E
T	R	U	R	K	U	P	A	M	L	H	L	Y
E	E	V	A	S	H	C	H	I	Q	N	A	R
N	O	R	M	U	T	Y	E	U	A	U	G	T
P	N	U	S	E	H	B	A	X	E	Q	I	N	R	C
S	O	Z	E	G	B	O	W	L	E	R	K	E	I	S
L	B	J	I	U	B	P	O	O	K	I	S	T	C	H
E	Z	N	F	O	U	R	X	N	R	E	T	S	O	F
M	O	V	A	L	Y	F	I	G	A	I	R	I	R	M
N	I	T	O	T	H	E	W	I	L	B	A	R	N	E
N	E	T	O	A	S	Z	S	O	M	B	R	E	R	O
R	A	Y	E	C	L	O	C	H	E	R	P	U	T	E
M	E	R	R	Y	O	U	T	I	M	E	S	T	S
		E	K	S	E	Q	B	I				

49

MIND GAMES

It's an odd silver-painted contraption decorated with screws, thumbtacks, ice-cream sticks, discarded spark plugs, and other odds and ends. It comes packaged in a papier-mâché "meteorite," and it brings messages of friendship from Mars.

You won't find this product in stores, however. The "Friendship Machine" was invented by a group of "Martians" from Schroeder Elementary School in Troy, Michigan, for an unusual competition: OM, or Odyssey of the Mind. Their task—to design, develop, and mass-produce an entirely new product within strict limits of time and cost—was just one of several challenges set by OM in 1985–86.

The OM competitions were begun in the 1970's by a group of educators who believed

that creative problem solving could open new doors for students. By working on problems, these educators felt, students would learn more than the basic facts of school subjects such as science, mathematics, history, and literature. They would learn to think more creatively. And in the process, they would have fun.

THE 1986 COMPETITIONS

By 1986, OM competitions were drawing entries from about 4,000 elementary, middle, and high schools in the United States and Canada. Teams from these schools worked through the school year to solve any of five long-term problems. They presented their solutions at local and regional competitions, where they were also faced with new, "spontaneous" problems that had to be solved by individual team members on the spot. Winners of the regional competitions went on to the World Finals, held in May, 1986, in Flagstaff, Arizona.

The teams were divided into three divisions: I (kindergarten through fifth grades), II (sixth through eighth grades), and III (ninth through twelfth grades). At all levels of competition, scores were determined by three factors: the team's solution to the long-term problem, their style—including the costumes and songs used, and the solution to the spontaneous problem.

Each team had an adult adviser—but, under the competition rules, no adult suggestions were allowed. Instead, team members had to work together to find their own solutions to the problems. And some of their solutions were creative indeed.

In the problem called **Bridging the Gap**, teams in Divisions I, II, and III built weight-bearing structures out of thin strips of balsa wood. This took some creative engineering because the requirements were exacting. Each team had to construct two structures that, together, would stand 8 to 8.5 inches (20 to 21.5 centimeters) high and would weigh no more than 25 grams. The balsa-wood strips had to be just an eighth of an inch (3 millimeters) thick.

In competition, the teams—dressed in

Bridging the Gap, Division I: Cedar Park and Edgewood Schools, Selma, Alabama

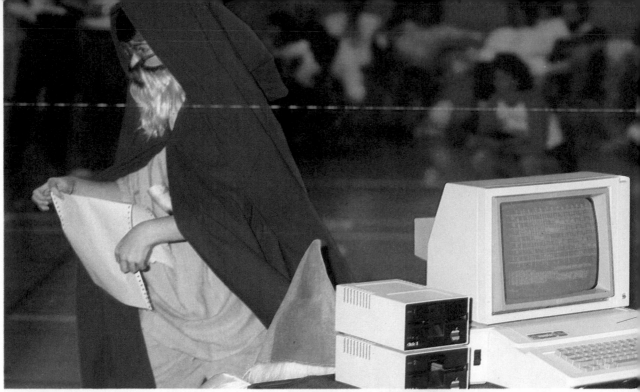

Treasure Hunters, Division II: Cook Elementary School, Richmond, British Columbia, Canada

History—The Way It Was, Division I (Joan of Arc): Star Hill School, Camden, Delaware

wild and fanciful costumes to show style— carefully piled weights on top of their creations, to see which could hold the most. A Division II team had the top weight in the eight minutes allowed for the test: an amazing 398 pounds (180 kilograms).

Teams in Divisions II and III tackled a computer problem called **Treasure Hunters**. Their task was to design a computer program that would guide team members through a 49-square grid laid out on the competition floor. Various items of "treasure" and a hazard were placed in different squares on the grid, but their exact locations weren't known until competition day.

On that day, each team was given ten minutes to modify its program and then, using information from the computer, send two treasure hunters through the grid to pick up or move the items. Each square on the grid could be entered only once, diagonal moves were forbidden, and each hunter could make only 25 moves. The other team members couldn't speak to the hunters or touch them. Instead, they used codes—such as flashing lights or flag signals—to tell them where to move next.

Imagination ran wild when it came to solving the problem **History—The Way It Was**.

Great Art Lives, Division I (*The Millinery Shop*): Hackensack Elementary School, Hackensack, New Jersey

Teams in all divisions chose from a list of ten famous historical incidents. Then, in a skit lasting ten minutes or less, they told both the standard story and their own humorous interpretation of what really happened.

For example, a Division II team from Fincastle, Virginia, showed Benjamin Franklin returning from the grave to give the "true story" of how electricity was discovered. Franklin said that he hadn't been conducting a scientific experiment—he'd actually made the discovery by accident as a child.

A team from Camden, Delaware, presented the story of Joan of Arc—as told by her dog. Naturally, it was the dog, not Joan, who was responsible for saving France during the Hundred Years War. In this version, the war was settled by a singing contest.

Great Art Lives made use of both artistic and dramatic talents. In this problem, teams painted or sculpted three works of art: two copies of works by a famous master (chosen from a list) and one in the style of that master. Then they brought one of the copied works to life in a skit, beginning or ending in the positions of the subjects in the painting.

For example, a Division I team from Hackensack, New Jersey, developed a story to fit Edgar Degas' painting *The Millinery Shop*. In their skit, the shopkeeper contemplated selling the shop, and the hats came to life one by one to convince her not to. Each turned out to have been worn by a famous person, and each sang a song. Another team, from Livingston, Montana, showed Paul Cezanne's *The Card Players*. In their version, Cezanne was painting the scene when an argument broke out among the players over whether a woman could join the game.

The "Friendship Machine" was one of the ingenious solutions to the problem called **Technocrats**. The Division I students who tackled this problem designed their products and production lines in advance. In competition, they were given ten minutes to produce ten reasonably identical products, package them, and place them on a shipping dock. Besides being new, the products had to work. Extra points were offered for finishing the products in less than the time limit and for using multiple components and a variety of materials. The teams also produced jingles and commercials for their products, and they dressed in costumes for the work.

"Teacher's Pet" was invented by students from Dagsboro, Delaware. And it was a pet no teacher should be without—an odd mechanical contraption that looked something like a dog. Equipped with chalk, foam and felt rollers, and a squirt gun, it could write on, erase, and wash chalkboards. It came packaged in a cage, with a piece of chalk for food.

A Division III team from Mendham, New Jersey, dressed in duck costumes to produce "Mr. Duck's Teach & Play," a toy for toddlers. It had a clock for a stomach, eyes that lit up, and a cloth covering with zippers and shoelaces to help young children learn how to dress. And a Division II team from Shorewood, Wisconsin, turned out the "Soggy Doggy Sanitizer." This product was an automated dog-washing machine assembled from a Styrofoam cooler. Each machine was packed with instructions and an order form for accessories (including goggles, earplugs, and a hairdryer for the dog). Commer-

cials included testimonials from celebrities and a jingle, the "Soggy Doggy Shuffle."

TAKE UP THE CHALLENGE

OM has come up with five more puzzlers for 1986–87. Students who take up the challenge will be asked to:

• Design and construct a vehicle that will fit into two suitcases, and then complete a set of tasks with it.

• Perform a set of tasks using energy from a chain reaction triggered by mousetraps.

• Design and construct a balsa-wood structure 9 to 11½ inches (23 to 29 centimeters) tall that weighs just 15 grams.

• Present a parody, satire, or analogy of a famous poem in the form of a skit.

• Create a performance of a scene that takes place in a cave in prehistoric times, showing an important discovery.

Whatever solutions the teams come up with, one thing is certain: Their answers will be creative, and they'll have lots of fun. Perhaps you and your classmates might like to take up the challenge too!

Technocrats, Division I (Friendship Machine): Schroeder Elementary School, Troy, Michigan

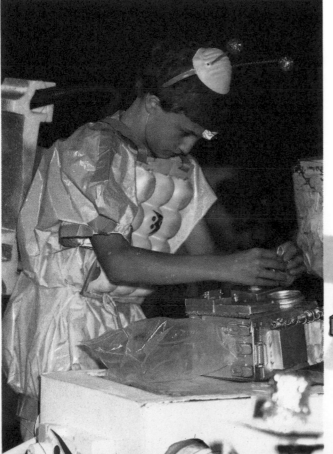

HAVE YOU HUGGED A PIG TODAY?

Pigs are no longer confined to the barnyard. Instead, they are turning up on T-shirts and greeting cards, in movies and cartoons, as car ornaments and belt buckles. People wear plastic pig snouts and hats with pig ears to parties, plant flowers in pig-shaped pots, decorate the walls of their homes with paintings and posters of pigs. In short, pigs are IN.

There's even a fan club for pigs—the Short Snout Society, whose primary objective is to improve the public image of pigs. To join, you have to take a Pig Aptitude Test. Once you're a member you can attend the Swine Ball and take part in other social events—including the pig-kissing contest at the Short Snout Gala.

Probably the biggest fans of these often maligned animals are those people who have pet pigs. Not just people who live on farms, but even people who live in cities and suburbs. They'll tell you that pigs aren't dirty, lazy, fat critters good only for eating, but are cute, cuddly, clean animals that can bring much pleasure into your life.

A LOT OF HOGWASH

Pet pigs may lead pampered lives, but many people still hold false beliefs about the animals. Some of this "hogwash" is even part of everyday language. You may, for instance, have called someone a "sweat hog" or said he "sweats like a pig." This is unfair. Pigs barely sweat—they can't, because they have few sweat glands. To cool off in hot weather, they have to lie in something wet. They would much rather wallow in nice clean water than in the gooey muck of a pigsty, but usually only the latter is available to them.

On the other hand, calling a stubborn person "pigheaded" *isn't* unfair. Pigs are quite willful and hard to deter when they want something. Like a chocolate chip cookie, perhaps. Pigs love sweets—in fact, they like all sorts of foods. One pet pig named Norma Jean eats whatever her owners eat, including clams, lobsters, and fancy hors d'oeuvres.

Unlike people, however, pigs don't overeat. Nor are they particularly messy eaters. "To eat like a pig" should be used as a compliment, not a criticism.

Pigs are among the most intelligent of all domestic animals, and they can be trained to do all sorts of things—pull wagons, chew bubble gum, carry banners that read "BOYCOTT BACON." In the 19th century one circus featured pigs that played "Yankee Doodle" and other songs on a xylophone. More recently, a woman in Houston, Texas, taught her pet pigs to swim. One of the pigs, a 3-month-old named Priscilla, became a heroine when she saved a boy from drowning in a lake.

Pet owners who have raised both dogs and pigs say that it's easier to housebreak a pig than a dog. They've even taught pigs tricks that are usually associated with dogs—such as how to sit, lie down, and roll over.

Pigs are curious animals and love to explore. Their favorite pastime is nosing, or rooting, about in the soil. They push the flat, leathery end of their snout along the ground like a miniature plow, unearthing anything in their path. They have a great sense of smell, too. The French have long taken advantage of these attributes to train pigs to sniff and root out truffles, rare fungi that grow underground and are considered food delicacies.

HOGGING OUR HEARTS

Throughout history there have always been at least some people who have been great admirers of pigs. Artists have captured the appeal of well-rounded pigs; poets have extolled their virtues; children have memorized nursery rhymes about them . . . and saved pennies in all kinds of piggy banks.

Perhaps the most famous literary pig is Wilbur, the friend of Charlotte the spider in E. B. White's story *Charlotte's Web*. On television there's the elegant Miss Piggy of ''The Muppet Show,'' and Arnold of the former ''Green Acres'' series (who likes to sip soda through a straw). Another popular actor is Porky Pig, star of numerous movie cartoons. And in newspapers you can follow the adventures of Salomey, Li'l Abner's beloved pet.

But these storyland pigs can't be snuggled up to while watching TV. You can't take them for a walk or for a drive in your new car. You can't hold conversations with them. And, as one pigmaniac says, ''You just haven't lived until you've kissed a pig!''

Pigs are in! And people who have them for pets say that they're cute, cuddly, and clean.

THE KIDDIN' KITTENS

"Quick, Marie! Hide!" whispered Berlioz to his sister. Both Aristokittens ducked behind one of the grand piano's heavy legs.

"Now!" Berlioz signaled. And both kittens began crying faintly.

O'Malley the alley cat came rushing into the music room, followed by Toulouse. The pitiful meows sounded as if they were coming from inside the piano.

"Ohmigosh!" panted O'Malley. "Those poor kittens! I've got to get them out!" He leaped up onto the piano bench, hooked his claws under the heavy piano top, and strained to lift it. When he had raised the lid a few inches, he called to Toulouse. "Quick! Get me something to prop it open!"

O'Malley struggled to hold the lid open. He looked back at Toulouse, who was trying to smother his snickers.

"Toulouse! Help me!" he yelled. Then he heard more giggling, coming from the piano.

O'Malley looked under the lid. No kittens. Then he looked around the piano. Suddenly the music room was filled with kittenish giggles.

"Hee-hee! Oh, Monsieur O'Malley! You were so funny!" Berlioz gasped, as he and Marie came out from their hiding places.

"Yes, we fooled you, didn't we?" added Marie.

O'Malley let the piano lid fall with a loud *bang!* The kittens stopped laughing. "So! You tricked me, did you?" he said sternly. "Toulouse, you told me your brother and sister were trapped in the piano. That wasn't a nice thing to do."

Berlioz was starting to giggle again. "It was just a joke—no harm done."

56

his back to the kitchen door. From the crunching sounds he was making, he was gnawing on something.

O'Malley leaped, spitting and snarling, and fastened his teeth on the dog's tail.

The hound squealed in pain, shook O'Malley off, and went howling down the alley. He left behind the bone he'd been chewing.

O'Malley looked at the bone. Surely it couldn't be all that was left of little Marie and Toulouse. Then he heard the giggles. Toulouse and Marie tumbled out from behind a trash can to join their brother Berlioz, who was laughing so hard he couldn't stand up.

"Oh, Monsieur O'Malley, you were so funny! We fooled you again, didn't we?"

O'Malley was too angry even to speak. He just glared at the kittens and stalked back into the house.

"I don't think much of your jokes," said O'Malley. And he stalked out.

"Oh, dear," said Marie. "I think we made him mad."

"He'll get over it," said Toulouse. "What will we do next?"

A little while later, Berlioz came skidding into the parlor where his mother Duchess and O'Malley were playing a game of chess. "Mama!" he cried. "Toulouse and Marie are in trouble! A big black dog has them cornered in the alley!"

"Oh, dear!" cried Duchess. "O'Malley! You must rescue them!"

O'Malley gave Berlioz a funny look, but he couldn't resist Duchess' appeal. "Let's go, kid," he said.

Berlioz led O'Malley out to the alley. Sure enough, a large black dog crouched there,

Later that afternoon, O'Malley and Duchess were discussing the kittens' behavior. "They're just going through a stage, O'Malley," said Duchess.

"Stage or not, Duchess, it has to stop. Why, if you had been there and seen that bone . . . you would've fainted, at least. Those three have to learn to tell the truth. This new game they're playing can be too cruel."

"You're right, of course," Duchess began. Suddenly they were interrupted by Roquefort the mouse, who hurried into the room.

"Duchess! O'Malley! Come quick!" he squeaked. "Marie is in trouble!"

"What has happened, Monsieur Roquefort?" asked Duchess.

"She has fallen into the well," explained the distraught little mouse.

"Let us go, O'Malley," said Duchess, heading for the door.

O'Malley put his paw out to stop her. "Wait a minute," he objected. "Where are her brothers?" He turned to Roquefort. "They've put you up to this, haven't they?" he inquired.

"Put me up . . . but Monsieur, Berlioz and Toulouse are in the garden. They are trying to keep Marie from drowning."

"Come on, old boy, you can admit it. Those kittens have been driving me crazy all day with their fake frights. Well, you can just tell them it won't work this time. Duchess and I have better things to do."

Then Duchess spoke. "Really, O'Malley, I can't imagine that Monsieur Roquefort would have anything to do with fooling us. Remember how helpful he was when Edgar tried to do away with us?"

O'Malley gave her a sour look. "Well, all right," he said. "Lead on, Roquefort. But those kittens better not be fooling again."

The sight that met their eyes when they got to the garden was a frantic one. Berlioz and Toulouse had lowered the well bucket to their sister. They were holding onto the rope, but they weren't strong enough to pull their sister out. O'Malley could see that the rope was beginning to fray several inches below the lip of the well.

Marie's choking, sputtering calls for help sounded all too real.

O'Malley told Roquefort to go get Frou-Frou, Madame's carriage horse. Meanwhile, he and Duchess held on to Marie's brothers to keep them from slipping down into the well, too.

Frou-Frou clattered into the garden.

"Take hold of the rope, Frou-Frou," urged O'Malley. "Your neck is long enough to reach it beyond the place where it's frayed. And you're the only one strong enough to pull up that bucket full of water and wet kitten.

"Pull back slowly, though, Frou-Frou," O'Malley cautioned. "We don't want to put any more stress on that old rope than we have to."

Carefully Frou-Frou grasped the old rope in her teeth. Slowly she backed up, little by little pulling Marie and the bucket up out of the well.

When the bucket was even with the edge of the well, O'Malley grabbed Marie by the scruff of the neck. He was just in time, for at that moment the rope broke, and the bucketful of water splashed back down into the well.

They all gathered around Marie, who shook herself to get the water out of her coat. Then she looked shyly at O'Malley.

"How can I ever thank you, Monsieur O'Malley?" she said. "Especially after those tricks we played on you."

"Now, now, my dear," he replied. "I'm just glad you're safe." Then he looked from one kitten to another. "But maybe this will teach you all a lesson," he added.

"Of course," Berlioz piped up. "Next time we want to fool you, we must get Monsieur Roquefort to help us."

O'Malley scowled at all three kittens. "If you think . . ." he began.

"No, no!" Berlioz was quick to say. "We have learned. I was only fooling."

BRINGING BACK THE WATERFRONTS

When towns and cities first began to grow up across North America, they were often located on natural harbors, rivers, and lakes. The reason was simple: Water provided a link with the rest of the world. Ships could bring goods, visitors, and news from outside and could carry the town's products to markets far away. Bustling waterfronts were often the busiest sections of cities in the 1800's. As rail and air travel became more important, however, many waterfronts fell into disrepair. Warehouses and factories became ramshackle, building lots stood empty, and piers rotted. People in the cities stayed away from the water.

But today, on the east and west coasts and on inland rivers and lakes, private groups and governments are getting together to bring the waterfronts back to life. Historic buildings are being restored. Boutiques and restaurants are being built. Parks are being carved out along the water's edge. Once again the waterfronts are bustling with activity—not as shipping depots but as places to shop, eat, live, and have fun.

San Francisco's Ghirardelli Square, housed in a building complex that was once a chocolate factory, was one of the first waterfront restorations in the United States. The work was done in the 1960's. Now the shops and restaurants in the 14 red brick buildings draw visitors day and night.

In Nova Scotia, Canada, a group of dilapidated historic warehouses on Halifax's harbor were saved from demolition. After a $10 million renovation project, the buildings are among the city's most fashionable addresses, with smart boutiques, offices, and restaurants.

Harborplace, built in the late 1970's, is part of a sweeping waterfront renovation project in Baltimore, Maryland. It includes 80 shops, 20 food markets, and 60 places to dine or snack—all housed in two airy, glass-enclosed pavilions overlooking the city's harbor. A famous ship, the U.S. frigate *Constellation,* is moored nearby and is open to the public as a museum. Elsewhere along Baltimore's harbor are a new world trade center, aquarium, and science center.

Entertainment especially for children and many other exciting events take place year-round—even in winter, on the ice—at Harbourfront, in Toronto, Canada. A broad promenade for strollers, joggers, and cyclists runs along the waterfront, past indoor and outdoor theaters, shops, restaurants, apartments, offices, marinas, hotels, and a museum.

Granville Island, on False Creek in Vancouver, Canada, was a decaying industrial area. Now it's home to theaters, an art college, shops, and restaurants. Shown is a popular shopping area: a public market for fresh meat, fish, and vegetables.

Faneuil Hall Marketplace, in Boston, celebrated its tenth anniversary in 1986. The centerpiece of the complex is Faneuil Hall (left), a historic colonial meeting house. Behind the meeting house are three long warehouse buildings packed with shops and restaurants. The center building, Quincy Market, has been restored to its original use as a food market, with stall after stall of tempting things to eat. Musicians, jugglers, clowns, and mimes entertain the crowds in the pedestrian malls between the buildings.

New York City's South Street Seaport is dwarfed by the skyscrapers around it, but the renovation can't be called small. Its focal point is the Fulton Fish Market, once a wholesale market for fish and now a place to buy all kinds of food. There's a seaport museum and six historic ships, including the bark *Peking* and the *Ambrose* lightship. Shops and restaurants are found in historic row houses and in new buildings, including a huge glass-enclosed pavilion that juts out over the East River. And, like the other restorations, South Street gives city people and visitors a chance to stroll along the waterfront and enjoy an outdoor snack.

FANCY FILES

Need a place to store magazines, school reports, or stationery? In very little time you can create fancy file boxes to place on top of your desk. All you need are cereal or soap boxes, colorful wrapping paper, and tape or glue.

There are two styles of files. To make a side-opening file, tape closed the top of the box and then cut out one of the narrow sides. For a top-opening file, cut out the top of the box; then cut downward at an angle on the two wide sides and across the connecting narrow side. To make sure the files don't tip over, place several strips of cardboard in the bottom of each box. Cover the boxes with wrapping paper. Tape or glue the paper in place.

Try making a matching pencil holder from a small tin can.

TAKE NOTE

Here's a note-taker just perfect for hanging next to your telephone. The doll holding this notepad is made from a small food strainer. The mesh part of the strainer forms the doll's face; the handle holds the notepad.

Begin by covering the mesh part of the strainer with a piece of skin-toned, stretchy fabric. Pull the fabric over the underside of the strainer until it forms a smooth surface. (Don't cover the hanging hook at the top.) With needle and thread, sew the ends of the fabric together in the back—over the strainer's open side.

Make hair from yarn and glue it around the top and sides of the face. Cut out eyes, a nose, and a mouth from felt and glue them onto the face. Make a felt bow and tie it around the neck. Now, use strong tape to attach the strainer's handle to the back of the pad of paper. And finally, tape two loops of felt onto the back of the notepad (at the bottom), and insert a colorful pencil.

THE PERFECTION OF FERNS

"Nature made ferns for pure leaves, to see what she could do in that line," wrote the 19th-century American author Henry David Thoreau. And indeed, leaves are what ferns are all about—delicate, feathery, intricate leaves, arching up from the ground. Ferns have no flowers to steal the show from their greenery; they don't need flowers to add to their beauty.

Ferns have another distinction: They were among the first plants to have proper roots

and leaves. The ancestors of modern ferns appeared some 300 million years ago. During the Mesozoic era—the age of the dinosaurs—ferns reached the size of tall trees. Ferns provided some of the vegetable matter that formed Earth's coal deposits millions of years ago.

There are still some treelike ferns, but the ones most of us know today are much smaller—3 feet (1 meter) tall or less. Still, ferns remain remarkable plants. Their method of reproduction—without flowers or seeds—is completely unlike that of most of the other plants we're familiar with. Their soft green beauty makes them a favorite of gardeners and woodland strollers. And, over the years, people have found many uses for these appealing plants.

ENDLESS VARIETY

There are about 10,000 different kinds of ferns. Together, they form an order called the Filicales. Ferns grow all over the world, anywhere that the ground isn't covered by ice year-round. But most ferns prefer warm climates, and most also need a great deal of moisture. For that reason, almost three-fourths of the fern species are found in the tropical and subtropical rain forests near the equator. Even in cooler climates, ferns usually prefer a moist and shady spot—along the banks of a forest stream, for example.

Most ferns plant their roots in soil. But some grow from cracks in rocks and stone walls, some grow in water, and some are air plants, or epiphytes. The epiphytes grow on the branches of trees and get their nourishment from damp air and from decaying matter that accumulates in the tree bark. One epiphyte, the oak or moss fern, grows on oak trees. It was honored by the Druids of ancient Britain, who held their religious ceremonies in oak groves.

In size, ferns range from minute to monstrous. Some ferns that grow in water are no more than a quarter of an inch (0.6 centimeter) tall and could easily be mistaken for bits of moss. At the other extreme are the tree ferns of South America and the Pacific islands. Some of these ferns grow 60 feet (18 meters) tall or higher, supported by strong, woody stems. They look rather like palm trees.

Ferns are noted for their delicate, feathery, intricate leaves, arching up from the ground. They come in a great variety of sizes and shapes, and their soft green beauty makes them a favorite of both gardeners and woodland strollers. Clockwise, from right: maidenhair fern; lady fern; shiny fan fern.

On the underside of a fern frond are clusters of spore cases—the secret to the plant's method of reproduction.

About 300 different species of ferns grow in North America. Apart from their size, they vary mostly in their leaves, which are called fronds. The fronds may be slender and tapering or wide and heart-shaped. They may be covered with fine hairs or scales. They are usually divided into many leaflets, and the leaflets themselves vary in shape from one species to the next.

Some plants that are often thought to be ferns are not, however. The "asparagus fern," which is often used in florists' arrangements, is really the flowering shoot of the asparagus plant. Resurrection fern,

which curls into a ball when dry and uncurls when wet, is actually a kind of spike moss.

HOW FERNS GROW

In most ferns, the fronds are the only part of the plant you see. The fronds rise on long stalks out of a rhizome, a sort of horizontal stem. Roots grow out of the rhizome to bring nourishment to the plant. Usually the rhizome is below the ground. Some ferns, however, have stems that travel above the ground or on other plants. And on the tree fern, the rhizome actually forms the trunk.

If you look at the underside of a full-grown fern frond, you'll probably see groups of brownish or whitish dots. These are clusters of spore cases, and they're the secret to the fern's method of reproduction. Each spore case is packed with microscopic spores. When the spores are ripe, the cases open and release them like fine dust into the air.

The spores fall to the earth. If they land in a spot with ample moisture and good growing conditions, they begin to develop into tiny plants. These plants look nothing like the ferns that produced them. They consist of single heart-shaped leaves, about a quarter of an inch across. In fact, the little plants aren't new ferns; they're just intermediate steps in the reproduction process.

The tiny plant is called a gametophyte ("reproductive plant") or prothallus ("first growth"). It develops special tissues that produce male and female sex cells (like the pollen and ovules in flowering plants). A female egg cell develops near the notch in the heart shape. Male sperm cells develop at the bottom point of the heart.

For the male cells to fertilize the egg cell, another ingredient is needed—water. When the little plant is covered with a film of moisture, the sperm cells swim across to reach the egg. This is why ferns like a moist habitat: Without moisture, they can't reproduce.

Once the egg has been fertilized, a new fern starts to grow, and the gametophyte withers away. In most ferns, the fronds emerge tightly coiled and uncurl as they grow. Coiled up, they look something like the head of a violin—and for that reason, they're called fiddleheads.

Some ferns have other ways of reproducing. One of the most unusual reproduction methods is that of the walking fern. When one of this fern's fronds touches the ground, it takes root and produces a new plant.

USES FOR FERNS

One of the simplest uses people have found for ferns is to eat them. Both the rhizomes and the new shoots, or fiddleheads, of certain varieties have been prized as delicacies in certain parts of the world, and the leaves of some types have been used to make tea. Today some supermarkets even carry fiddleheads, fresh (in season) or frozen.

In times gone by, people also made medicine from ferns. Several types of maidenhair ferns, native to North America and Europe, were used to make cough syrups and similar medicines. Oak fern was used against arthritis as well as respiratory problems. Wall rue, a common European fern that grows in rock crevices, was thought to cure swollen glands. The American Indians made a tonic from the rhizome of the common lady fern, and they treated snake bites with a poultice made from the roots of the rattlesnake fern. A concoction made from the root of the male fern is still used in many countries to rid people and animals of intestinal parasites.

Ferns were also used to make a primitive sort of shampoo, said to be especially good for preventing baldness. Sweet-scented dried ferns were included in potpourri and sachets. Bracken, a common fern that grows along roadsides and in open areas in Europe and North America, was used as bedding for farm animals and thatched roofing for houses. In medieval times, ash from burned bracken was used as an ingredient in glass and in soap. The reason the ashes were used was that they were high in alkali, which is necessary for both materials.

People also entertained some strange beliefs about certain ferns. Wall rue, for instance, was fed to cows to ward off evil spells that might sour their milk.

GROWING FERNS

Today ferns are valued mostly for their beauty. They are favorites in shady gardens, as houseplants, and in florists' bouquets. The Boston fern, the maidenhair fern, and the holly fern are some of the types often seen in gardens.

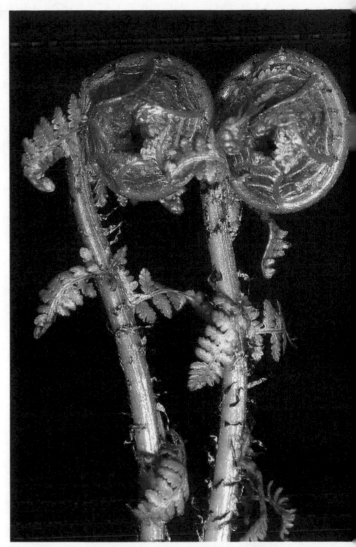

The tightly coiled fronds of a new fern resemble the head of a violin, and that's why they are called fiddleheads.

The trick to growing ferns is to duplicate their natural habitat as closely as you can. Tropical ferns and epiphytes can be difficult; they need special conditions that are best provided in a greenhouse. But ferns that are hardy outdoors where you live will do well if they have a shady, moist spot in your garden. Indoors, they need moderate sunlight and plenty of water. Regular fertilizing will help keep your ferns growing. They'll reward you with masses of delicate green fronds, so that you can have a bit of woodland beauty in your home.

WHY ANIMALS DO WHAT THEY DO

Before the first astronaut rocketed into space, a chimpanzee named Ham led the way. Early in the U.S. space program, Ham was strapped in a capsule and sent into orbit. When he returned to Earth, he was grinning. The ground crew thought that Ham was pleased with his space ride, but the chimp knew better. That smile on his face wasn't really a smile at all.

An animal's behavior doesn't always mean what it appears to mean. Actions that seem similar to human actions may in fact be very different. When a chimp smiles, is it happy? When a snake flicks out its tongue, is it going to sting an enemy? When a raccoon washes food, is it practicing habits of good sanitation? Scientists who study animal behavior have come up with some surprising answers to these questions.

A full, open grin is usually shown by a chimp who is frightened. It is often accompanied by loud screaming.

WHY CHIMPANZEES SMILE. When a person smiles or frowns, you usually know what it means. The human face expresses a wide range of moods and emotions. The face of a monkey or ape expresses many emotions, too—but it's easy for a human observer to be fooled.

A British scientist named Jane Goodall studied the facial expressions of wild chimpanzees in Africa. As she watched the animals, she learned to recognize feelings like fear, anger, joy, and frustration in a chimp's mobile face. For instance, if a chimp is angry or intends to attack, it presses its lips together tightly. If it's in a friendly mood and wants to be groomed by a companion, it purses its lips and pushes them forward in a pout. In the chimpanzee's world, a pout is both a greeting and an invitation.

When a chimp opens its mouth, pulls back its lips, and shows its teeth, it appears to be smiling or grinning. But its grin isn't a sign of pleasure. Instead, a grinning chimp reveals fear. A chimp grins during and after an attack, or when it's threatened by a stronger chimp. Grinning is almost always accompanied by loud screaming. History doesn't record whether Ham the astrochimp was screaming when he landed on earth, but his wide grin showed clearly that he was scared out of his wits.

If a chimp keeps its teeth closed when it grins, it is more nervous than frightened. This kind of grin is accompanied by squeaking sounds and whimpers. A low-ranking chimp approaches a higher-ranking one by displaying a closed grin, which is very much like a nervous smile in a human.

A chimp does have a genuine smile, what Jane Goodall called a "play-face." When a chimp is happy or having fun, it opens its mouth, juts out its chin, and shows its lower teeth. This play-face is accompanied by grunting sounds, or chimpanzee laughter.

WHY WOLVES HOWL. Once heard, the haunting sound of wolves howling on a moonlit night can never be forgotten. There have always been legends and superstitions about those wild, spine-tingling howls that seem so eerie and sinister. Are the wolves baying at the moon? Are they closing in on a deer or warning human listeners that it's time to climb a tree? What do the howls really mean?

Wolves actually have a number of calls. And they don't just howl when the moon is out, or even at night. As a rule, a pack of wolves will howl together every evening, moon or not, and again in the early morning. Pack howling is always started by one wolf. The animal shapes its mouth carefully, closes its eyes, and utters a long, low, moaning sound, which rises higher and higher. Then the other wolves join in, each with its own distinct voice, producing the wild harmony that seems to fill the wilderness. Usually the performance lasts about 30 seconds, but it may continue for a minute or more. As each wolf stops howling, it may bark sharply.

A group howl seems to be connected with the pack's hunting territory. Many animals utter calls and cries on their home territory, warning rivals to keep their distance. A wolf pack will defend its territory against other packs, and howling is a way of proclaiming property rights. If wolves of a neighboring pack are within hearing, they will answer the howl—but they will also keep away.

When a single wolf howls alone, it seems to be calling to the rest of the pack. Usually, its fellow wolves will answer. By howling, individual pack members can keep in touch with each other and signal their positions when separated.

Howling may have other meanings, too. It's quite possible that wolves enjoy howling together simply because they're glad to be together.

WHY RATTLESNAKES RATTLE. Is anything more frightening than the sound of a rattlesnake rattling in the wilderness? First you hear a sound that resembles the rapid clicking together of dried bones. As the rattler shakes its tail faster, it sounds more like the angry buzz of an insect or the hiss of escaping steam.

That sound doesn't mean that the rattler is about to attack. A rattlesnake shakes its tail to warn away enemies and give itself time to escape. Its rattle can save the snake from being stepped on by a horse, or attacked by a dog. A rattler would rather rattle than fight.

A pack of wolves will howl together to proclaim their hunting territory. When a single wolf howls, it is usually trying to make contact with the rest of the pack.

If possible, a rattlesnake will always move away from danger by slithering into a hole or behind a rock. But if it's cornered or taken by surprise, then it may strike and bite without rattling. People are bitten because they step on rattlesnakes, get too close, or try to pick one up.

A baby rattlesnake has no rattle. All it has is a small hard "button" at the tip of its tail. The first time it sheds its skin, it loses its baby button and gains its first real rattle. From then on, it gets a new rattle every time it sheds its skin. Each rattle is a dry, hollow scale connected loosely to the scales on either side.

To warn away enemies, a rattlesnake makes a fearsome noise by shaking its tail. To smell, a snake flicks its tongue in and out to pick up odors from the air and ground.

Since a rattler may shed its skin several times a year, you can't tell its age by counting its rattles. Also, it may lose some of its rattles as it squeezes between rocks or hooks its tail on twigs. And it may shake its tail so hard, it actually shakes off a rattle or two.

Strangely enough, a rattlesnake can't hear its own rattle. Snakes have no ears, and they can't hear sounds as we do.

WHY SNAKES FLICK OUT THEIR TONGUES. A snake's tongue is often called a "stinger," but it doesn't sting. The tongue is harmless to other creatures but very important to the snake.

All snakes have a keen sense of smell. They smell in two ways—with their nostrils and with their tongues. When a snake slithers along flicking out its dark forked tongue, it's testing the air and ground for odors, much as a dog sniffs along a country path.

A snake's flicking tongue picks up odors from the air and the ground. Then the tongue carries the odors inside the snake's mouth. On the roof of its mouth are two pits, called Jacobson's organs. When the snake presses its tongue against these pits, it can both smell and taste every odor its tongue has picked up. Its tongue helps it to hunt, find other rattlers, and stay away from trouble.

WHY ELEPHANTS TAKE MUD BATHS. An African elephant may be ten feet high and weigh six tons, but when it wallows in the mud it seems as playful as a puppy. A whole group of elephants will join together in a riotous mud bath. They'll sit in the mud, lie down at full length, roll on their backs, and wallow about noisily. That's why a muddy area visited by elephants is called a wallow.

Mud can be comforting on a hot afternoon. It feels cool and soothing, and it relieves itching. And when the bath is over, the coating of mud protects the elephant's hide from the hot sun and from annoying insects and parasites. Elephant hide is an inch thick in places, but it's very sensitive, especially to fly and mosquito bites.

WHY RACCOONS WASH THEIR FOOD. The raccoon is called "the washer" because it seems to wash its food in water before eating. Away from streams and lakes, it eats all sorts of fruit, grains, and small creatures without bothering to wash them. But when a raccoon is near water, every morsel is washed and scrubbed until there would seem to be no flavor left.

A raccoon's favorite hunting grounds are shallow pools along the banks of streams. It digs under rocks, gravel, and sand, and whatever it fishes up is sloshed, dunked, and scrubbed repeatedly before being eaten.

Is the raccoon being sanitary? Not really. In fact, it isn't washing its food at all. It's actually hunting for small water creatures. As it probes and shifts the sand and gravel, it rolls every handful between its nimble black fingers until it finds what it wants—a tasty crayfish, mussel, or snail. Then it pops the creature into its mouth and starts "washing" again.

WHY OPOSSUMS "PLAY POSSUM." An opossum is small, shy, and seemingly defenseless. It has no special armor to protect itself or weapons to fight with. But it does have a special trait that helps it survive and flourish.

When an opossum is cornered, it falls on its side and lies absolutely still with its eyes closed and its tongue hanging out of its mouth, just as though it were dead. Its heartbeat slows down. It may actually be in a state of shock caused by fright. If picked up, the opossum is as limp as a rag. It can be

When a raccoon appears to be washing its food, it is actually hunting for small water creatures.

carried about by its tail for some time without moving before it suddenly comes "alive" again. That's how the expression "playing possum" originated.

A baby opossum will "play dead" the first time it faces danger, even if it has never seen another opossum behave that way. The act is an instinct, and it's very effective. An attacking animal, after a few sniffs at the "corpse," will usually move away. A few minutes later the opossum will come to life, shift position, look cautiously around, scramble to its feet, and scamper away.

Playing dead is a common defensive technique among many insects, reptiles, and birds, and among a few other mammals. The jackal, the honey badger, and the striped hyena all "play possum."

WHY DUCKLINGS FOLLOW THEIR MOTHER. When you walk through the park on a spring day, you sometimes see a platoon of ducklings waddling single-file behind their mother. They'll follow her wherever she goes. They've been doing that since the day they hatched.

The urge to follow is a powerful instinct among newly hatched ground birds like ducks, swans, chickens, geese, and turkeys. These birds are able to stand up and run around soon after they hatch. Usually they start to follow their mother. But if for some reason their mother isn't around, they'll look for something else to follow.

Farmers noticed this behavior a long time ago. If a farmer takes a newly hatched ground bird from its mother and keeps it with him long enough, the baby bird will try to follow him. If it is returned to its mother, it doesn't seem to recognize her. It will still run after the farmer.

An Austrian scientist named Konrad Lorenz was the first to investigate this following instinct. He hatched some goose eggs in an incubator, and after they hatched he conducted some experiments. He found that newly hatched goslings will run after the first moving object they see. It may be their mother, or it may be a person, a dog, a rolling ball, a toy car, or almost anything else the goslings see moving away from them. And after following something for just a brief time, they'll refuse to follow anything else.

This following instinct is strongest during the first few hours of a gosling's life. If a newly hatched bird is kept in a room by itself and isn't given a chance to follow, it gradually loses the urge to follow. At the end of only one day, it hesitates and seems fearful of anything that moves. At the end of two days, it won't follow at all.

Dr. Lorenz called this behavior *imprinting,* because a baby bird's first impressions seem to become so deeply imprinted in its mind. By following its mother, a newly hatched gosling learns to recognize her and associate with others of its kind. But if it follows a farmer and accepts him as its mother, then it may want to associate with humans for the rest of its life. Such a bird has become imprinted to humans.

Imprinting is important in the lives of other creatures as well. Hoofed animals like cows, sheep, and deer also struggle to their feet and start to walk a few minutes after they are born. Ordinarily, they follow their mother. In this way they learn to recognize her and stay with the rest of the herd. But if a hoofed animal is taken from its mother and raised on a bottle by humans, it will learn to follow humans. A bottle-reared lamb becomes so strongly attached to humans, it will "baa" plaintively when left alone with other sheep. If it is forced to return to its flock, it will go off by itself to graze and may stay apart from the flock for the rest of its life. That's why Mary's little lamb followed her everywhere she went.

RUSSELL FREEDMAN
Author, *Animal Instincts*

Above: The small, shy opossum has a special trait that helps it survive—it "plays dead." Below: Newly hatched ground birds such as swans follow the first object they see—usually their mother. This is how they learn to associate with others of their kind.

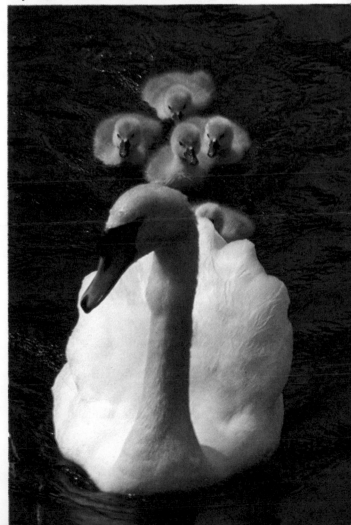

THE SWEET SUCCESS OF SMELL

New mown grass . . . a cake baking in the oven . . . the first daffodils of spring . . . the spicy scent of a Christmas tree. These aromas probably make you feel warm and happy all over. Did you ever wonder why?

People often think about what they see or hear, but rarely about what they smell. And scientists have only recently begun to study the sense of smell, the oldest and deepest of our senses. What they've learned so far, however, is leading them to recognize smell's true importance. Smell, it seems, is closely linked to our emotions—and perhaps to our health. Some doctors are even exploring aroma therapy, using scents to help treat a variety of medical problems.

HOW YOU SENSE A SCENT

When you see something, your eyes register patterns of light. When you hear something, your ears pick up sound waves. And when you smell something, your nose detects chemicals—odor molecules that are given off by the item you're smelling.

When you sniff a flower, for example, odor molecules rise through your nostrils to the back of your nose. There, the molecules are absorbed by the membranes and microscopic hairs that line the nasal passages. One small patch of this nasal lining—called the olfactory epithelium—is packed with nerve cells that are stimulated by odors.

As soon as the odor molecules hit, these cells fire off signals along direct nerve pathways to the brain. The signals are received in the brain's olfactory bulb, a small area just behind the eyes. From there, the signals are carried deeper into the brain and the odor is identified.

The sense of smell is closely linked to the sense of taste. In fact, many of the flavors we "taste" in food are really aromas. Odor molecules enter the nose as we lift food to our mouths, or they enter through the back of the mouth, where the nasal passages connect with the throat. Many distinct flavors, such as coffee and chocolate, can't be detected when the sense of smell is blocked.

Some scientists think that the human sense of smell evolved to its present state long before the rest of the human brain developed. Our sense of smell, they say, basically isn't much different from that of a fish. And some animals have more highly developed smell centers than ours. The part of a dog's brain that is concerned with smell, for example, is much larger than the part of the human brain that does the same thing. And a dog's sense of smell is much sharper than a human's.

Still, the human brain is capable of distinguishing more than 5,000 aromas, although most people can't give a name to even half that many. Newborn infants react to odors, and babies just a few days old can smell the difference between their mothers' milk and that of other mothers. The ability to tell one odor from another is thought to peak in adulthood, between the ages of 20 and 40. After age 70, it declines. But scientists don't know how the brain tells one scent from another. One theory is that the receptor cells in the nasal passages are specialists—certain cells are stimulated only by certain aromas.

MEMORY AND EMOTION

Another aspect of smell that scientists are only just beginning to learn about is its relation to other brain functions, such as memory and emotion. The link between smell and memory is found in many animals. For example, scientists were long puzzled by the way ocean salmon manage to return each year to the streams where they were born, in order to breed. The answer was the sense of smell: Every stream has its own distinct odors, and the fish were able to smell their way back home.

People remember smells longer and better than they remember sights and sounds. If you hear a song on the radio, you may not be able to place it when you hear it again several months later. But if you smell an aroma you've once smelled before, chances are you'll remember what it belongs to and also how that item looked, tasted, or felt.

You'll probably even be reminded of where you were and how you were feeling the first time you smelled that scent. That's one reason why certain odors make you feel good—the scent of daffodils, for example, reminds you of a warm spring day. Your sense of smell can remind you of unpleasant experiences as well as happy ones. In one research study, students smelled a particular odor while they were told they had scored poorly on a test. Later, when they smelled that odor again, more than half of them felt unhappy.

Many manufacturers make use of this aspect of the sense of smell when they market their products. Cleaning products, for example, are often given lemon or pine scents because people seem to associate those scents with cleanliness. And, even when they aren't linked to specific memories, certain smells seem to bring out emotions in people. The scent of almond, for instance, makes people think of happy events. Peach, strawberry, and apple scents seem to help people relax.

The reason for smell's close link to memory and emotion may lie in the make-up of the brain itself. Nerves travel from the olfactory bulb to distant points throughout the brain—including the centers for memory and emotion. Researchers who placed dye in the scent-sensitive nasal passages of animals found that the dye was carried all the way to these areas by the nerve cells. Thus, when you smell a flower, your memory and emotions are stimulated automatically.

AROMA THERAPY

For many years, people have thought that certain scents had medical properties. Mint, for instance, was supposed to be a stimulant. Lavender was said to cure headaches. Eucalyptus was supposed to prevent sleep. Now researchers are finding that some of these beliefs may be more than folklore, and aromas may actually play an important role in medicine.

Some smells, particularly spiced apple, have been shown to lower blood pressure and reduce muscle tension. They may be used to help people deal with stressful situations or to treat high blood pressure. And the scent of peaches seems to ease pain and may also help control panic attacks and epilepsy.

Other scents have been found helpful in controlling appetite, depression, and migraine headaches. Some aromas help people get to sleep, and others seem to wake them up. One researcher has even invented a scent alarm clock that sends a mist of wake-up aroma out into the room.

One day, odors may even be used to deliver drugs to the brain—to treat neurological diseases and serious mental disorders such as schizophrenia. Usually, drugs circulate in the blood and pass through the blood-vessel walls to reach body cells. But in the brain, a membrane called the blood-brain barrier surrounds the blood vessels and prevents the drugs from getting out. That means that the brain cells can't be reached by most drugs. Now researchers are looking for ways to link drug molecules to odor molecules. By hitching a ride with the odor molecules, the drugs may be able to act directly at sites of disease deep within the brain.

Such medicines are for the future. Scientists are still studying the role of smell in health. Meanwhile, you might want to do some research into your own smelling power.

TEST YOUR SMELL POWER

How sharp is your sense of smell? Can you sniff out the difference between chocolate and cherries? Between tunafish and tomatoes?

Your nose may not be as sharp as you think it is. Researchers say that people's sense of sight often prejudices their judgment when it comes to identifying odors. In other words, if you see a rose, you expect it to smell like a rose—and when you sniff it, it does.

It's easy to test your sense of smell. Ask a friend to help you. Put on a blindfold, and then have your friend hold different substances under your nose—ketchup, spices, onions, fruit, cheese, and other foods; toothpaste, soap, and similar household items; flowers and plants from the garden.

Most people can identify about 70 percent of all odors, the researchers say. If you can do better than that, you may have the makings of a great nose!

THE CAPITAL OF SCENT

If you visit Grasse, in southern France, the first things that strike your eye may be the fields of flowers that surround the city. And the first thing that strikes your nose may be the aroma of those flowers—jasmine, roses, narcissus, lavender, and others—carried by the warm Mediterranean breezes.

Grasse is a city that scent made famous. It's the center of the French perfume industry, which is known the world over. The land and the sunny climate of the region make it the perfect growing spot for flowers, and since the 1600's flowers have been grown there specifically for perfume.

The flowers are hand-picked in the early morning, when their scents are freshest and strongest. Then, through a long distilling process, they are reduced to scented oils. It takes 4,000 pounds of rose petals to make a pound of rose oil—and that pound of oil may sell for more than $1,500.

A fine perfume is made by blending different floral oils with aromatic chemicals and alcohol. It takes a keen nose to develop such a blend, and the master perfumers of Grasse are known for their noses. At schools run by the perfume industry, students are taught to distinguish some 1,500 aromas. The top professionals—the master "noses" —can identify as many as 3,000 at first sniff.

Today perfume makers are relying more on computers and laboratory equipment to make their blends. To keep costs down, some are also using artificial scents and less expensive floral oils from North Africa and other regions. But the flowers of Grasse are still prized above all others, and this city remains the scent capital of the world.

Neon is glowing again, in advertising signs . . .

NEON—NEW AND NIFTY

Streaks of hot pink and electric blue light up the night sky, pulsing and blinking in rhythmic patterns. It's not an invasion from outer space—it's neon. Once looked down upon as the ultimate in poor taste, neon signs are enjoying a dazzling revival today.

Neon signs first made their appearance about 1910, when a French inventor perfected a technique for making them. The basic element in a neon sign is a long, thin glass tube, carefully heated and bent by hand to whatever shape the sign maker wants. All the air is sucked out of the tube, to create a vacuum. Then the tube is filled with neon, a colorless and odorless gas. (The name "neon" is from the Greek word meaning "new." It was given to the gas in 1898 by its discoverers, the British chemists Sir William Ramsay and Morris W. Travers.)

Neon has a remarkable property: When electricity is passed through the tube, the gas glows in brilliant colors. Pure neon glows a bright red. By adding other gases or by coloring the tube, the sign maker can produce other colors. A few drops of mercury, for example, produce a vivid blue.

From the 1920's on, neon signs popped up all over North America and around the world. They advertised theaters, restaurants, nightclubs and casinos, car dealers, hotels, and countless individual products. At night, downtown shopping areas glowed with unearthly light as neon signs flashed and blinked to attract people's attention. Many signs even showed animated figures that seemed to move as different neon tubes went on and off.

By the 1950's, neon signs were becoming less popular. Many people thought the bright colors and flashing lights were in poor taste.

Neon signs were also expensive to maintain, and they were easily damaged by the weather. Businesses turned to other ways of making signs that would light up at night— fluorescent bulbs placed behind sheets of plastic, for example.

Some businesses, however, continued to use neon signs. And some areas remained famous for their signs. The casinos in Las Vegas, Nevada, for example, have huge and elaborate neon signs that turn night into day. New York City's Times Square and Tokyo's famous shopping district, the Ginza, are other areas that are well known for their nighttime signs.

But today people are looking at neon signs in a new way—as an art form. The brilliant colors and bent glass tubes of a neon sign can create striking forms and patterns that just can't be duplicated in other ways. Neon advertising signs are being displayed in art galleries. And artists are also using neon tubing to create works that have nothing to do with advertising.

Neon has become the subject of books and of articles in art magazines. It's been used in

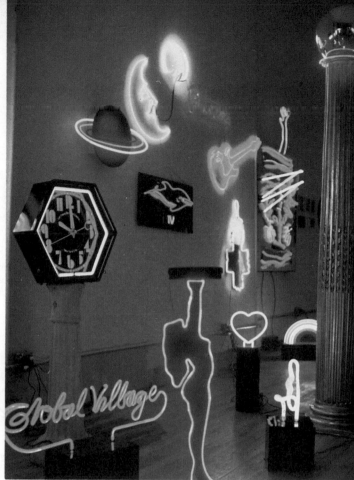

. . . and in art studios.

stage productions, such as the Broadway show *Sophisticated Ladies,* to create the feeling of past eras. It's been used to present the future, too: In science fiction films, neon lights are often used to represent lasers and other space-age weapons.

With improved materials and computers to synchronize the flashing of the signs, businesses are also returning to neon. Some restaurants and stores are bringing the glowing advertising tubes indoors, where they serve as decorative accents.

All this has created a lot of work for sign-making companies. Since neon signs can't be mass produced, the companies have had to train new workers in the delicate art of forming the glass tubes. Also, while vibrant new neon works are being created, some people are trying to save and preserve the best and most famous of the neon signs of the past— so that they can keep glowing right into the future.

A Pup Of
A Different Color

"Come on, Fluffy! Hurry, Ruffy! Scooter! Let's investigate!" Scamp burst out of the doghouse as fast as his legs would carry him, while his brother and sisters tried to keep up with him.

Scamp raced for the trash cans, which were full of bright wrapping paper and ribbons from Darling's birthday the day before.

"Maybe there's some birthday cake left!"

"I don't know if we should do this, Scamp," argued Scooter, but Scamp was tugging at a piece of ribbon. In an instant, the trash can came toppling over with a crash and a clatter.

Scamp's brother and sisters hid behind a bush while Jim Dear rushed outside and found Scamp sheepishly sitting in a pile of trash, a birthday bow hanging around his neck and a squashed piece of birthday cake between his paws.

"I should have known it was you, Scamp.

You seem to have a nose for trouble," Jim Dear exclaimed, as he picked up the trash. "See if you can keep out of mischief for the rest of the day. All right?"

Scamp crept away, joining his brother and sisters in the bushes.

"You'd better be more careful," Ruffy told Scamp.

"I will," the mischievous pup promised. And then he let out a gasp.

"Oh, look!"

All eight eyes turned up toward the side of the house, where a long ladder was propped.

"It's a burglar!" exclaimed Scamp. "Let's get him!" He started to run toward the house, but Fluffy stopped him.

"Wait a minute," she told him. "It's broad daylight. Mother's inside and Father's around here somewhere. If it's a burglar, they'll stop him."

Scamp wasn't sure, so he watched more intently. Soon a man wearing overalls came walking around the house. In his right hand was a large brush; in his left hand was a bucket of paint.

"He doesn't look like a burglar," suggested Ruffy.

But Scamp was unconvinced. "I think I'd better get closer, just to find out."

"Hold on there, laddie." Scamp's neighbor, Jock the Scottie, came strolling through the yard. "He's no burglar, of that I'm sure."

"Nope. Looks like he's here to paint the house," explained Trusty, the bloodhound, who was at Jock's side.

"Trusty's right, Scamp."

Scamp turned around and saw his mother, Lady, standing behind him. "And I think you pups should stay as far away from that painter as possible. Scamp, I heard you've been in enough trouble for one day."

"Oh, Mom!" wailed Scamp. But Lady gently herded her pups away from the house.

Fluffy and Ruffy went off to chase a butterfly, while Lady returned to the house. Scamp was left alone behind the hedge, watching the painter put a fresh coat of paint on the stately Victorian house.

"Care to join me for a stroll down to the Park?"

Scamp turned around and was surprised to see his father, Tramp, standing behind him.

"Gee, thanks, Pop. But I think I'll stay right here and watch the painter," Scamp explained.

"Suit yourself," Tramp replied. "Sounds pretty dull to me."

"I'm supposed to be good today. Jim Dear says I have a nose for trouble."

"Well, sometimes a nose can get you into trouble, it's true. But sometimes, it can get you *out* of trouble, as well. Just take care, kid." And Tramp trotted away.

Scamp quietly watched the painter all day. Finally, the sky began to darken and the painter packed up his brushes and went home, leaving the long ladder leaning up against the house. Several cans of paint were left behind, too.

"He's gone at last!" thought Scamp.

Just then, he heard Darling calling the pups to dinner.

"But I'll have to come back later," Scamp thought as he hurried off to join his family.

After dinner, Lady tucked her pups into the doghouse for the night and gave them a goodnight lick. The lights in the house were dark and everyone was fast asleep, except for Scamp. As soon as the coast was clear, he dashed toward the house.

Scamp was delighted to see that there was a full moon shining down on the yard like a bright spotlight. He could see the cans of paint sitting side by side. "Oh, boy!" he thought. "Now I can really investigate!"

As he sniffed away at the first paint can, the lid fell off and he saw that the paint was yellow—just like the new paint on the house. Suddenly, his ears began to twitch as he heard footsteps approaching. Fearful that Jim Dear was about to catch him in the act, Scamp scurried behind the nearest bush.

In the moonlight he saw a man, but it definitely wasn't Jim Dear. It wasn't the painter, either. The man was dressed in dark clothes, and he wore a black mask. He looked around nervously. Then the strange man began to climb the ladder toward the open window.

"Uh-oh!" said Scamp to himself. "This isn't right!" The fur on Scamp's back stood up straight, and he burst out of the bushes, barking as loudly as he could.

The man looked down in surprise. A light went on in the house and the man slid down the ladder. When he reached the bottom, Scamp nipped at his heels and the man stepped right into a can of paint. It tipped over with a loud crash. Scamp felt a shower of paint covering his body. But the strange man was gone!

By the time Scamp could see through the yellow paint, both Jim Dear and Darling were staring down at him. Neither of them looked very happy.

"Who is this yellow dog?" asked Jim Dear.

"I'm afraid it's our Scamp," Darling answered, biting her lip.

Scamp whimpered softly, but Jim Dear was angry. "Now I have to clean you up— in the middle of the night!" he exclaimed. "And then, you'll have to be punished!"

By the time Jim Dear had scrubbed all the yellow paint off Scamp, the morning sunlight was peeking through the big trees. Jim put Scamp on a rope and marched him outside, past the ladder and the puddle of spilled paint. Suddenly Scamp looked down at the ground and let out a loud yelp!

"Oh, be quiet, Scamp," said Jim Dear, impatiently. But Scamp planted his feet firmly on the ground and stopped dead in his tracks.

"What's wrong with you?" asked Jim Dear. Then he looked down and saw exactly what Scamp saw: bright yellow footprints from a man's shoes leading from the spilled paint can across the yard and into the street.

"This is a matter for the police!" cried Jim, hurrying back into the house.

Just then, Tramp strolled into the yard. "What's up, pup?" he asked.

Scamp gulped hard. "I think Jim Dear is going to send me to jail!" he exclaimed.

"What? Oh, Scamp, come on!"

"Well, I spilled this paint last night and now he's calling the police!"

Tramp hung around until Officer Moran arrived on the scene. Jim Dear pointed out the yellow footprints leading away from the house.

"Someone must have tried to break in here last night," Jim Dear explained to the police officer. "And Scamp scared him away!"

Scamp barked three times to let him know the story was true and Officer Moran hurried off, following the footsteps.

"What I think you need, Scamp . . ." began Jim Dear. Scamp closed his eyes, waiting to hear the punishment. "What you need is a nice, big breakfast!" And Jim Dear picked Scamp up and took him into the house.

It wasn't long before Officer Moran arrived back at the house with the good news. He had followed the bright yellow footprints to a shack several blocks away, where he found the would-be burglar hiding. The shack was full of loot the burglar had stolen from other people in the neighborhood!

"He's in jail now," announced Officer Moran. "But we would never have found him if it weren't for the clever trap this fellow set!" He bent down and gave Scamp a pat.

"That's what I always say: Scamp here has a nose for trouble!" Jim Dear bragged.

Scamp saw Tramp watching. He looked just as proud as Jim Dear and gave Scamp a great big wink.

A HATFUL OF FLOWERS

"Plant" a country garden on a straw hat! The hat can be worn or hung on a wall in your room. It also makes a charming gift.

You need a straw hat, ribbons, and a variety of dried leaves and flowers—you can buy these or dry them yourself. It's easiest to work with a glue gun, which can be purchased at a craft shop.

Begin by making a bow with long streamers. Center the bow on the back of the hat or set it on one side; then glue it in place. Try positioning the leaves and flowers in different ways. When you're completely satisfied with the arrangement, carefully glue the pieces to the hat.

THE BUMPY RAINBOW

Debi Thomas is a special kind of figure skater. No, Debi Thomas is a special kind of person.

Her skating accomplishments speak for themselves. In February, 1986, at Uniondale, New York, the 18-year-old Californian turned in a dazzling performance to win the U.S. women's championship. The following month, in Geneva, Switzerland, she out-leaped and out-scored the best of the rest and was crowned the new world champion.

But there are other things that make Debi Thomas special. For one, she is the first black skater ever to win a major individual title. For another, Thomas is a full-time college student. While her skating competitors devote themselves entirely to the sport, Thomas is a pre-med student at Stanford University. Her major is medical microbiology, and she plans to be an orthopedic surgeon when her skating days are over.

As for being the sport's first black champion, Thomas is matter-of-fact. "I never really thought about that too much," she said. But when it comes to studying and training, Thomas is far from matter-of-fact. She attends classes from 8 A.M. to lunch, hits the ice until early evening, and then hits the books—sometimes until 3 A.M. It's a difficult schedule, and success has been hard-won. Said Thomas after winning the U.S. championship: "I went through a lot to get here, and it feels good. This is like the pot of gold at the end of the rainbow, but it was a bumpy rainbow."

The rainbow began in Poughkeepsie, New York, where Debi was born. Her parents, both computer programmers, moved to California, and Debi was raised in San Jose. When she was 3½, her mother took her to see the Ice Follies. Debi was enchanted and begged for a pair of skates. She got them at 5, and at 9 she won her first figure-skating competition. The following year, her mother hired Alex McGowan to be her coach. (He's worked with Debi ever since.) To be near McGowan's ice rink, Debi enrolled in San Mateo High, about 45 minutes from home. Time was tight and so was money. Debi sewed her own skating dresses and usually competed in worn-out skates.

In addition to her perseverance and athletic ability, one quality that's helped Thomas rise to the top is her love of performance. "The more people the better," she says. "I get fired up and put more into it." A prime example was the U.S. championships. She had skated poorly in practice, unable to execute the five triple jumps in her program. Once in front of the crowd, however, Thomas was transformed. Her confidence grew as the cheering grew, and she landed every jump flawlessly. "When you kind of amaze yourself I think it helps the program," said the young champion.

Debi Thomas has amazed a lot of people.

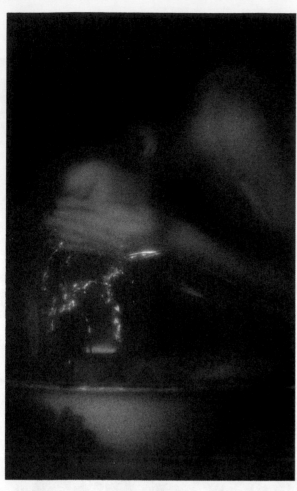

YOUNG PHOTOGRAPHERS

 Spots on a giraffe . . . stripes on a shirt . . . a delicate tracery of leaves. Line and pattern can be captured by the camera so we can see them in new ways. Sometimes all it takes is an eye for composition and a little thought. Sometimes darkroom wizardry—hand-coloring and other techniques—turns an everyday photograph into a work of art. Either way, the results can be extraordinary. A photograph can evoke the gentler time of a bygone era or the neon vibrancy of today's hectic world.

 The young people who took the pictures shown on these pages were among the winners in the 1986 Scholastic/Kodak Photo Awards Program. The program offers scholarships and other awards to high school juniors and seniors in the United States and Canada.

Face Splash,
**by Jennelle Marcereau, 17,
Mt. Clemens, Michigan**

Stretch,
**by William Fornwalt, 18,
Chesterfield, Missouri**

Reticulation, by Ann Laienski, 16, Elk Grove, California

Electric Ghosts, by Jennifer Laskin, 18, Mayfield, Ohio

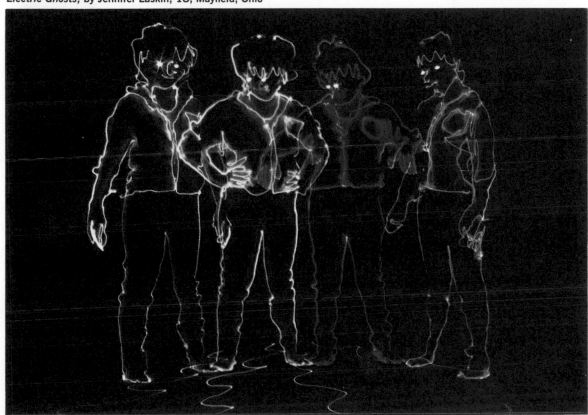

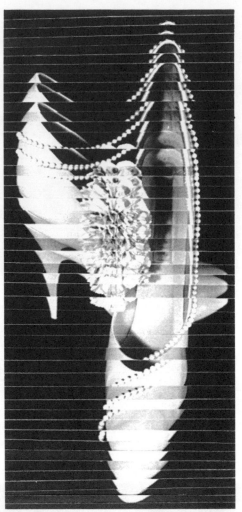

String Along,
by Lisa McDonald, 17,
Chesterfield, Missouri

Balloonrise,
by Eric Thun, 17,
DeWitt, New York

Studying,
by Lurline Tau'a, 14,
Waianae, Hawaii

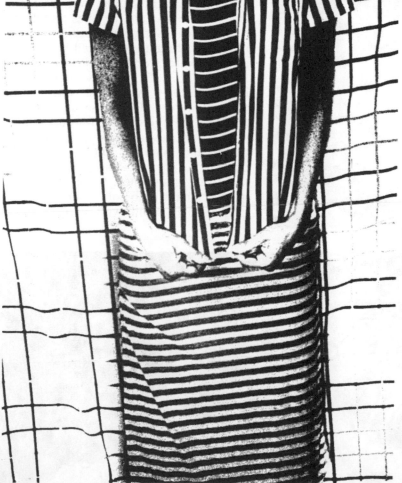

Untitled,
by James Whitcome Riley, 15,
South Bend, Indiana

93

Sea anemone

Angelfish

Psychedelic dragonet

UNDER-WATER-COLORS

Far more vivid than any watercolors in an artist's paintbox are the hues found beneath the tropical seas. Intense reds, brilliant blues, and bright greens and yellows create an underwater world that vibrates with color. Much of this fantastic variety of shades is produced by the animals that live in the tropical waters. But these animals haven't taken on their colors just for decoration.

There are several reasons for the dazzling colors and patterns. One is camouflage—color helps protect a fish or another sea animal from its enemies. On land, camouflage usually means drab colors such as brown or gray, which blend with earth, trees, and

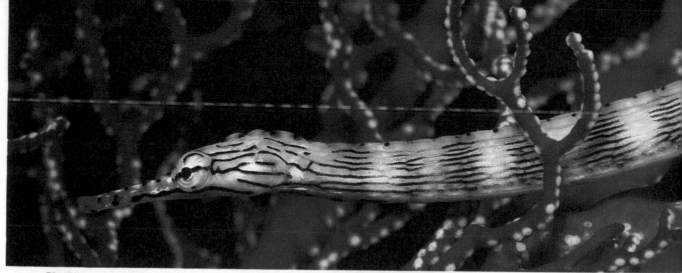

Pipefish

rocks. But in the tropics, from the Caribbean Sea to the Indian Ocean, the coral reefs and marine plants are usually brilliantly colored. Thus bright colors and stripes and spots help sea animals stay hidden.

The animal that sports vivid coloring may also be warning predators that it is poisonous. An octopus that attacks a brilliant red fish and gets stung with poison will remember that fish's pattern and color—and avoid it. Color also helps sea creatures identify others of their species at mating time. The tropical reef is crowded with hundreds of different species of fish, crabs, and other sea animals. Still, males and females of each species manage to find each other to mate—thanks to the distinctive colors that mark each one.

But whatever the reasons for these fabulous under-water-colors, the result can be summed up in one word: beautiful.

Spotted grouper

LADY LIBERTY: RADIANT AT 100

*Here at our sea-washed,
    sunset gates shall stand
A mighty woman with a torch . . .*
                    Emma Lazarus
                    "The New Colossus"

On July 4, 1986, hundreds of boats—from rubber rafts to Navy battleships—jammed New York Harbor. Thousands of people lined the shore. Above, blimps, helicopters, and jet fighters buzzed back and forth. As darkness fell, the sky exploded in the biggest fireworks display in U.S. history—40,000 skyrockets, bursting into showers of red, orange, yellow, blue, and green.

The reason for all this excitement? The country was celebrating the 100th birthday of the Statue of Liberty, the noble lady who towers more than 300 feet (90 meters) over the harbor. The statue, properly called *Liberty Enlightening the World,* had been given to the United States by France and dedicated in 1886. The hundred years that followed had brought a lot of wear and tear, and the statue had been given a multi-million-dollar face-lift in time for the anniversary.

All this money and attention wasn't showered on the statue just because it's one of the world's largest. Nor was the reason the fact that the statue represented an engineering triumph in its day. Those were important aspects—but much more important was what the statue stands for: the concept of freedom that has been central to the United States since the nation was founded. Standing at the entrance to New York Harbor, the statue was the first bit of America that millions of immigrants saw. Liberty, with her torch held high, welcomed them. She became a symbol of the hope they shared for a better life in a new land.

HOW THE STATUE WAS BUILT

The idea for the statue was first suggested at a dinner party in France, in 1865. The host, historian Édouard-René Lefebvre de Laboulaye, was a great admirer of the United States and its democratic form of government. At the same time, he chafed under the rule of France's emperor, Napoleon III. As de Laboulaye saw it, the statue would serve two purposes: It would be a magnificent gift marking French friendship and admiration of liberty; and it would be a subtle way of showing disapproval of the emperor's dictatorial regime. The sculptor Frédéric Auguste Bartholdi was among the dinner guests, and he was just the man for the job. Bartholdi, 31, had a taste for monumental works, and he took to the idea immediately.

Originally, the statue was to have been a gift for the United States' 100th birthday, in 1876. But for various reasons, building it took much longer than expected. De Laboulaye, in fact, never saw it—he died in 1883. But Bartholdi and others carried the project through.

In 1871, Bartholdi traveled to the United States to choose a site for the statue. He found it in New York, on Bedloe's Island (now Liberty Island), a small bit of land at the entrance to the harbor. "Here, my statue must rise," he said, "here where people get their first view of the New World." With a picture of the site clearly in his mind, he went home to work on the statue.

The first step was a plaster model 4 feet (1.2 meters) high, completed in 1875. It presented Liberty as a Greek goddess, dignified and stern. In her right hand, she held aloft a torch—symbolizing enlightenment and freedom. In her left, she held a tablet (inscribed with the date July 4, 1776), symbolizing the Declaration of Independence and the rule of law. On her head was a crown with seven spokes, standing for the seven continents and the seven seas. At her feet were broken shackles, symbolizing release from tyranny. The artist's mother is said to have been the model for Liberty's face.

What was most remarkable about the statue, though, was the scale Bartholdi planned for the work. It would stand 151 feet (46 meters) tall. The face was to be 10 feet (3 meters) wide; the waist, 35 feet (10 meters) around; the index finger, 8 feet (2 meters) long. For lightness, the completed statue would be hollow, made of thin copper sheeting. Even so, it would weigh 450,000 pounds (204,000 kilograms).

Holding this colossus together presented enormous problems in engineering—it would have to bear not only its own weight but also the forces of wind and weather. Nothing like it had been built before. Bartholdi turned to Alexandre Gustave Eiffel, the engineer who would later build the Eiffel Tower in Paris. Eiffel designed an interior iron framework for the statue. The copper exterior was to be attached to it by a system of iron struts and bars.

Bartholdi made progressively larger plaster models, refining the design as he went along. His final model was 36 feet (11 meters)

high. He then cut this model into sections and carefully enlarged each one to full size. When the sections had been modeled in plaster, carpenters carved wood molds to fit over them. Then metalworkers hammered thin sheets of copper into the molds to form the final statue pieces.

Only the torch was ready in time for the U.S. centennial celebration in 1876. It was displayed in Philadelphia and caused quite a stir. When the head was completed in 1878, it was erected in Paris. For an admission fee, people could walk up and look through the 25 windows in the crown. In this way, Bartholdi helped raise money for his work; he also had models of the statue cast and sold to raise funds.

Piece by piece, the statue rose in Bartholdi's Paris work yard, looming over the city. By 1884, the last piece had been put in place. Then the statue was taken apart, packed into

The Statue of Liberty, before restoration. For 100 years, she has represented the "inner meaning" of America.

crates, and shipped across the Atlantic. It arrived in New York City in the spring of 1885.

In the United States, there were other problems. France was giving the statue, but America had to provide the pedestal for it to stand on. A committee had been formed to raise funds for the pedestal, which would be designed by Richard Morris Hunt. At first, there wasn't too much support. But after the newspaper publisher Joseph Pulitzer organized a major fund-raising campaign, the American public came up with the money. The granite pedestal, together with the eleven-pointed, star-shaped base, raised the statue to a total height of just over 305 feet (93 meters).

Finally, on October 28, 1886, the statue was ready to be dedicated. Ships and boats filled the harbor. President Grover Cleveland and officials from France and the United States gave speeches honoring U.S.–French relations. Bands played patriotic tunes. Then Bartholdi unveiled the statue, and Liberty's torch was lit.

A BEACON FOR IMMIGRANTS

From the start, the statue captured people's imaginations. Liberty holding her torch aloft appeared in paintings and stories, and poets wrote sonnets to her. The most famous of these poems, "The New Colossus," was written by Emma Lazarus in 1883, to help raise funds for the pedestal. Its words expressed the idea that the statue quickly came to symbolize:

"Give me your tired, your poor,
Your huddled masses yearning to breathe free,
The wretched refuse of your teeming shore.
Send these, the homeless, tempest-tost to me,
I lift my lamp beside the golden door!"

To thousands of immigrants, Liberty stood for refuge from poverty and oppression—a new chance in a new country. They came from every port in Europe, crossing the ocean in crowded ships. Many died on the way. But for those who made it to New York, the statue was their first sight.

One immigrant described what it was like: "Mothers and fathers lifted up the babies so that they too could see, off to the left, the Statue of Liberty. This symbol of America—this enormous expression of what we had all been taught was the inner meaning of this new country we were coming to—inspired awe. . . . Not until the last nightlight died out did these watchers—Armenian, Greek, Turk, Italian, French, what not—go below."

Beginning in 1892, many of these immigrants entered the United States at the U.S. Immigration Station on Ellis Island, also in New York Harbor. They passed through the station at a rate of 5,000 a day. The station's vast, white-tiled Great Hall echoed with the sounds of many languages. Most of the immigrants were on the island just a few hours, for medical and legal examinations. A few were detained, and about two percent were turned back because they were ill or because of legal difficulties.

By 1954, patterns of immigration had changed. People were more likely to arrive in the United States by plane than by ship, and more immigrants were arriving in the South (from Latin America) and the West (from Asia). Ellis Island was closed. But in

all, 12,000,000 people had passed through it
—so many that today, more than half of all
Americans have at least one ancestor who
arrived there.

Emma Lazarus' poem, meanwhile, had
achieved new stature. In 1903, it was placed
on a plaque inside the statue's pedestal. And
within a few years, its famous lines were permanently linked with the statue in people's
minds.

MANY MEANINGS

Immigrants weren't the only people who
found special meaning in the Statue of Liberty. Posters and songs about Liberty helped
drum up patriotic feelings during World War
I, and soldiers returning from the war were
welcomed by the statue's beacon.

Over the years, various people and groups
used Liberty to make statements, both personal and political. Bereaved families scattered the ashes of loved ones from the top of
the statue. In 1956, the year of the Hungarian
uprising against Communism, Hungarian
demonstrators hung their flag below the statue's torch as a symbol of their desire for
freedom. In 1971, demonstrators took control of the statue for two days to dramatize
their opposition to the Vietnam War.

But a lot of people really took liberties
with the statue. In 1883, Mrs. Cornelius Van-
derbilt appeared at a costume ball dressed as
the Lady. The next year, a laxative manufac-
turer offered $25,000 for the pedestal fund if
its name could be placed on the pedestal for
a year. The offer was turned down, but
within a few years pictures of the statue were
appearing regularly in advertisements for
everything from matches to lemons. Liberty
was shown dressed in the latest fashions to
advertise fabrics, and pouring soap into the
harbor to advertise cleaning products. A pig
striking the statue pose advertised a hog
remedy. Liberty also appeared on souvenir
spoons, candlesticks, tie clips, and thimbles.

But all the commercial uses to which the
statue was put never detracted from its most
important message. The Statue of Liberty
continued to be a much-loved symbol of the
"inner meaning" of the United States. Over
the years, millions of people climbed the 171-
step spiral stairway that winds through the
hollow statue to the crown, to pay tribute to
Lady Liberty.

Restoration began, and towering scaffolds rose around
the statue. The project was called "the job of the century."

RESTORING THE STATUE

Gradually, time took its toll on the statue.
Parts of the framework were weakened by
stress. The torch leaked. The right arm,
which had originally been mounted incor-
rectly, shifted so that one point of Liberty's
crown hit the arm and dented it. Insulation
between the copper skin and the iron bars
that held it in place crumbled away. Where
the metal pieces came in contact with each
other, they began to corrode. Salt air and
pollution scored the surface of the statue and
quickened the corrosion inside.

By 1982, the statue was in a sorry state. The U.S. government, looking ahead to the centennial, appointed a commission of private citizens and gave it the job of restoring the statue. The commission was also to restore the facilities on Ellis Island, which had fallen victim to weather and vandals.

The first step was to raise money for both projects, and the commission appealed to everyone from schoolchildren to major corporations to donate. Eventually, some 20,000,000 individuals and companies responded and sent more than $280,000,000.

Towering scaffolds rose around the statue, and hundreds of workers climbed up to begin the restoration. It was, as one worker put it, "the job of the century." Inside the statue, nearly every one of the almost 1,800 iron bars holding the copper skin was removed and replaced with a stainless steel bar. Warped struts were also replaced. Seven layers of paint and two layers of coal tar were stripped from the inside of the copper. The right shoulder was strengthened, the

viewing area in the crown was improved and given new windows, and the stairway was widened.

Outside, the seven spokes of the crown were removed, refurbished, and set back in place. New copper pieces were made for parts of the nose and hair, where corrosion had destroyed the original. The new pieces were carefully colored to match the soft blue-green patina of the old copper. But many of the streaks on the statue couldn't be removed, so they were left in place.

The torch, which had undergone a number of renovations over the years, was removed completely. It was replaced with a new torch, made by a team of French artisans who traveled to the United States for the job. They worked with the same techniques that Bartholdi had used in his original design (which had been changed before the statue was dedicated in 1886). The flame of the old torch had windows and was lit from within. The new torch was made of copper, and its flame was covered with gold leaf—which in

The old torch, whose flame had windows and was lit from within, was completely replaced. The new torch has a flame covered with gold leaf and is illuminated by a ring of outside lights.

A fleet of tall ships from countries around the world paraded up and down the Hudson River—a highlight of the July 4, 1986, birthday celebrations.

the sun would gleam brightly, and at night would be illuminated by a ring of outside lights.

The pedestal was repaired and given a new elevator. Inside the base, an existing museum on immigration was expanded. And Liberty Island itself got a new docking area and pedestrian mall. Plans for Ellis Island included restoration of the old buildings to house a museum and exhibit areas. But this work was scheduled to be completed by 1992, in time for Ellis Island's anniversary. Meanwhile, everyone worked overtime to make sure that the statue was ready for its party in 1986.

THE CELEBRATION

The statue's birthday party lasted four days. On Thursday, July 3, Warren Burger, the chief justice of the U.S. Supreme Court, gave the oath of citizenship to several hundred immigrants on Ellis Island. Thousands more, in other cities, were sworn in at the same time. Then U.S. President Ronald Reagan, joined by French President François Mitterrand, relit the statue, bathing it in colored lights. A short time later, Reagan rekindled the torch.

The next day, July 4, President Reagan reviewed a flotilla of Navy warships in the harbor. Then a fleet of windjammers, tall ships from countries around the world, paraded up and down the Hudson River. In the evening came the spectacular fireworks show—ten tons of explosives let loose in less than half an hour. The bursting rockets were accompanied by a rousing concert broadcast on radio and television.

On July 5, the statue was reopened to the public, and hundreds of people lined up to see it. Others toured the tall ships and navy vessels in the harbor. Meanwhile, a harbor festival in lower Manhattan offered food and entertainment to the thousands of people who had come to New York City. The festival continued through Sunday, when the party ended with a huge show at Giants Stadium, across the Hudson River in New Jersey. The show featured thousands of performers.

Some people thought all the hoopla over the statue was too much—that with all the fun, people would forget what the statue stood for. But Liberty was no stranger to celebrations. Through it all, the statue gazed out toward the sea, the new torch shining as an unforgettable symbol of the ideals that are most important to Americans.

COMPUTER BULLETIN BOARDS

"For Sale: 10-speed bike; new tires. Best offer."

"Is anyone out there taking computer classes at the community college? I'd like to talk to you."

"Missing! 8-year-old collie named Shaggy. Reward."

"50's dance at Rogers H.S. Friday night, beginning at 8. Bring your parents' old dance records."

These messages and ads are just like the ones on the bulletin boards in your school and in the local supermarket—except in one very important way. Instead of being written on paper and posted on corkboard, they appear in glowing letters on a computer screen. They're on a computer bulletin board, one of the newest ways to communicate with other people.

A computer bulletin board is an electronic "warehouse" for messages—messages are actually stored in a computer's memory. If you have the right equipment, you can contact the computer to read the messages. You can also contact the computer to have your own message "posted" on the bulletin board, for other users to read.

KINDS OF BULLETIN BOARDS

Some bulletin boards are set up by individuals, churches, clubs, schools, small organizations, and other such groups. These bulletin boards are generally local and free. That is, they are open to anyone who calls in.

Other bulletin boards, such as those within corporations and government agencies, are private. Codes or passwords prevent outsiders from gaining access to private boards.

Still other bulletin boards are part of commercial information networks such as The Source and CompuServe. To use these boards, a person must subscribe to the network and pay a fee.

Some computer bulletin boards are small, devoted to specific subjects, such as computer games, genealogy, airplanes, jokes, food, astronomy, and dating, to name just a very few. Other boards are so large that they are divided into subject categories. Callers who connect with such boards are offered a choice of message lists—each one covering a different subject.

New bulletin boards are constantly springing up, so it's difficult to know exactly how many are in existence. But there are at least 2,500 public bulletin boards across the United States. The New York City area alone has more than 100 boards, with names both straightforward and strange-sounding—Board of Ed, NY Computer Society, Time Tunnel, Coco Creations, The Worm Hole.

To learn about bulletin boards in your area, check computer publications or ask local computer retailers. Many bulletin boards provide telephone numbers of other boards. Once you've contacted one board, you may become part of a whole new world.

USING BULLETIN BOARDS

Do you want to read the messages on a computer bulletin board? Or leave messages of your own?

To do so,

you need a computer, a modem (a device that connects the computer to a telephone), and communications software (a program that will allow your computer to "talk" over the telephone lines). You also need the telephone number of the bulletin board you would like to reach.

Turn on your computer, load the communications program, and dial or key into the computer the phone number of the bulletin board. When the bulletin board's main computer answers the phone, you'll hear a tone that tells you that your computer is connected to it. The bulletin board computer may send a welcoming message, which will appear on your screen. Next, it may ask whether you want to read messages on the board or add a message of your own.

If you want to add a message, you simply type it on your computer and then tell your computer to "send" it through the modem and telephone line to the bulletin board. You'll be asked if your message is for retrieval by anyone or only by a specific person. If it's for a specific person, you need to know the name that person uses. Some people use their real names when communicating through a bulletin board. Others use nicknames or codes, such as "Fat Cat" or "VX-27."

Let's say a computer game has you flummoxed. You just can't figure out how to escape from "jail." You call up a bulletin board and leave a message for anyone to read: "How do I get into the guard's house or past the oooga-oooga lady?" Leave your name, too—or a code name, such as "Red Rody." Later, check to see if there are any messages for you. If another player knows the game and reads your message, he or she may send you a private message: "Red Rody, look for a pilot's license in the mailbox near the guardhouse."

BECOME A "SYSOP"

The person who runs a computer bulletin board is called a system operator, or "sysop." Many sysops are teenagers.

Sysops usually leave their computers turned on 24 hours a day. People can contact the computers and leave messages even if the sysops are elsewhere.

To set up a bulletin board and become a sysop, you need a computer, a modem, and a bulletin board software package. This type of software can be purchased from a computer store. Some bulletin board software is in the public domain, which means it's available free (usually through computer clubs and similar groups). And if you know computer programming, you can write your own software. Which is the best choice for you? Why not ask for help on someone else's bulletin board?

JENNY TESAR
Designer, Computer Programs

This appliquéd marriage quilt from the early 1800's is filled with hearts, a universal symbol of love. The heart was a traditional design in the folk art of colonial America.

HEART TO HEART

The folk art of America from the 1700's to the late 1800's depicts a variety of traditional designs. The heart—a universal symbol of love, courage, friendship, hospitality, and fidelity—is one of the most enchanting.

Traveling artists painted hearts on dower chests and birth and baptismal certificates. Young girls stitched and embroidered hearts on samplers and quilts. Tinsmiths pierced hearts in foot warmers. Potters etched them on presentation plates. Puritan stonecutters carved hearts on gravestones, and carpenters and craftsmen carved out and drew hearts on furniture, including chests and chairs. Ironmongers wrought heart shapes on kitchen utensils, and sailors carved hearts

on whales' teeth during their long voyages in search of the great sperm whales. Hearts were glazed onto stoneware, woven into coverlets, and cut out from paper.

All these products of brush, kiln, loom, needle, and scissors were necessary objects. But they were decorated to please the eye of the maker and to kindle feelings in the beholder. They were the personal expressions of men and women—folk artists who were by nature, rather than by training, masters of their craft.

The heart was a traditional, symbolic design. Most often, it was used in folk art connected with the major events of life: birth, marriage, and death. Most of the decorated objects were found in the home. Many were used for "best" or for "company." They became family heirlooms, carefully saved generation after generation. All these objects now provide us with a record of a design form and of an entire way of life.

HEART HISTORY

The simple heart, with its bold form and appealing grace, is an ancient design with hazy origins and a fascinating history. It has roots reaching back 20,000 years: A great heart was found on a painting of a mammoth in the caves of Cro-Magnon man. Almost every ancient religion and culture throughout the world has given the heart important symbolic meaning. Chinese, Hindu, Judaic, Christian, and Islamic religions all viewed the heart as the center of life, the soul or spirit of a person. Thus the heart became a symbol related to the worship of God.

The heart shape as we know it today can be found in Egyptian art dating from the 14th century B.C. It was part of the distinctive decoration painted on Egyptian coffins. Later, hearts appeared on Coptic (Egyptian Christian) embroidery—possibly as religious symbols. It is the Egyptians who have been credited with bringing the heart form to Europe, in the A.D. 500's.

The Middle Ages (from the 500's to the mid-1400's) witnessed a dramatic evolution of culture, art, and language throughout Europe. From this period there are scattered clues as to the directions that the heart design would take in later folk art.

The heart representing the love of God was used in the ornamentation and architecture of cathedrals and in paintings and sculpture. When Parisian cardmakers, at the end of the 1300's, introduced the first set of playing cards using the now familiar suits—hearts, diamonds, spades, and clubs—each suit was thought to represent one class of medieval French society. The hearts were associated with the church.

Germans and other northern Europeans adopted the heart on their cards but chose

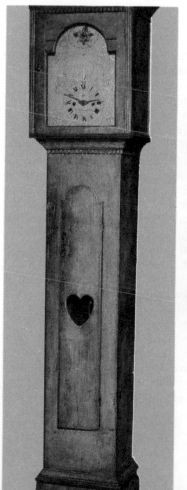

Everyday items for the home were decorated with hearts by tinsmiths, potters, stonecutters, quilters, ironmongers, carpenters, and weavers. They carved hearts out on furniture, glazed them onto stoneware, and fashioned them into kitchen utensils.

bells, leaves, and acorns for the remaining suits. Their selection reflects a different tradition, in which the heart is one of several symbols associated with growth, fertility, and regeneration. The heart, the source from which all things grow, became in later folk art a symbol of Mother Earth.

The romantic medieval tradition of courtly and chivalric love began using the heart as a symbol by the 1100's. In the 1100's and 1200's, the heart was associated with romantic love in French ballads that told of troubadours offering their hearts to fair maidens. The red heart appears in a 15th-century French illuminated manuscript called *The Book of Love*. The heart was also found on woven carpets, on carvings in ivory, and on jewelry boxes of this period.

In the Renaissance, philosophers and scientists focused on the brain as the center of thinking and reasoning, and on the heart as the center of the emotions. Martin Luther

and John Calvin, leaders of the Protestant Reformation, both adopted the heart in their seals.

By the 1700's, people had gained a new degree of independence and wealth, allowing them to decorate their homes and objects of daily use more richly. And they adopted familiar and traditional designs, perhaps copying without understanding the meaning of the religious symbols of the past. Thus the heart became as much associated with love between people as with God's love. It appeared on painted furniture, textiles, embroidery, and other objects. In many European countries, it became associated with the traditions and customs surrounding courtship and marriage.

HEARTS IN AMERICA

In America, the early settlers carried on the traditional use of this design. As early as 1674, a gravestone cutter carved a heart on a tombstone in Charlestown, Massachusetts. A blacksmith cut out a heart, a cloverleaf, and the date 1682 on a banner weather vane that stood on the roof of the second meetinghouse in Lynn, Massachusetts. But America's folk art—and the heart design—flowered after the Revolutionary War. And particularly after 1820, the heart became an increasingly sentimental design, associated with romance and friendship.

To the immigrants from Switzerland and Germany who settled in Pennsylvania, the heart was an image of love with faint overtones of religious meaning. The Pennsylvania Germans (or Pennsylvania Dutch, as these settlers were sometimes called) developed the tradition of Fraktur—documents in ink and watercolor with decorative lettering and ornamental designs. The most common type of Fraktur was the birth and baptismal certificate, but other examples include rewards of merit, house blessings, bookplates, religious texts, and valentines. The heart was often drawn on the borders of certificates, and used as a central design surrounding vital statistics or a religious text. Many of the unknown Fraktur artists were rural schoolmasters. But there were also important Fraktur artists, known for their distinctive handling of the heart design.

Large and small hearts appeared in em-

The Pennsylvania Dutch often used hearts in their Frakturs —documents in ink and watercolor that combined decorative lettering and ornamental designs.

broidered samplers (done to show mastery of various stitches) from many parts of the country. Quilts, especially bridal quilts, were often decorated with hearts. Paired or intertwining hearts, representing marriage, were a common design, as were combinations of a heart with paired birds and a single or double heart pierced by an arrow. Heart-shaped wreaths of vines or flowers signified a blessing and protection of the home. The "heart and hand" was another popular design in textiles, particularly in quilts. It was associated with "giving one's hand in marriage" and also with friendship.

Country furniture was often enlivened with paint or simple carving. Thus the heart appears on the chests, chairs, beds, and tables of that time. And even country homes would have appeared empty without pictures on the walls. Watercolor-and-ink family records were a popular art form in the late 1700's and early 1800's, and a number of artists incorporated hearts in their basic designs for these works. One such artist, who became known as the "heart and hand" artist, drew family records decorated with hearts and hands in the borders framing them.

Boxes were made from materials at hand —wood, tin, whalebone, cardboard, and papier-mâché—and came in every size and shape. Their broad, flat sides provided superb surfaces for decorations, which often included hearts. Little hand-whittled and carved heart-shaped boxes, small enough to fit in the palm of a hand, were made as love tokens. Heart-shaped key plates surrounded the keyholes of boxes. And heart-shaped bandboxes carried the "theater caps" of fashionable women to an evening at the opera or theater. At the theater, the woman would remove her tall bonnet and replace it with the smaller cap.

Many kitchen utensils had hearts wrought, carved, or incised into the patterns that decorated them. In some cases the hearts were purely decorative; in others, the heart was featured as a symbol of love and pride. It was customary in Pennsylvania German families for the parents to give their daughter for her dowry a fork, spatula, and taster, each decorated with a heart. Tin cookie cutters with the heart-and-hand design and the simple heart mold were used mainly at

Christmas and Easter by these families, and strung together and hung in the attic when not in use.

The custom of giving hand-decorated love letters replete with hearts and lovingly written verse was introduced in America by the Pennsylvania Germans around 1750. If sent on February 14, these letters were considered valentines. The most common were circular, cutwork love letters, created by folding a piece of paper and then skillfully scissor-cutting a design on the folded edges. The true lover's knot—a continuous labyrinth forming intertwining hearts—was introduced in the first decade of the 1800's.

Early valentines and love letters are also found outside Pennsylvania. Small, intricately designed hearts, hearts and hands, or heart and key designs were often created by young girls and boys to be given as tokens of love and esteem to friends and teachers. Whether on love letters, valentines, or love tokens, the heart symbolized true feeling, the most treasured of human emotions.

from *Folk Hearts*
CYNTHIA V. A. SCHAFFNER and SUSAN KLEIN

Captain Hook's Flying Scheme

Captain Hook rubbed his lantern jaw as he paced the deck of his pirate ship. "I must find a way to get rid of Peter Pan and take over Never Land," he muttered to himself.

Hook raised his spyglass and caught a glimpse of Peter Pan flying, arms outstretched, with his friends Wendy and John and Michael. A tiny star glittered close to them. It was Tinker Bell, the pixie who sprinkled them all with pixie dust so they could fly. They all zoomed through the sky, swooping over treetops and shooting through clouds.

"If only I could fly!" grumbled Captain Hook. "I wouldn't waste the power having fun. I'd make my ship and crew fly, too. We'd take over Never Land! Mermaid Lagoon, the Indian Village, Hangman's Tree—they would all be mine! And the first thing I'd do would be to order Peter Pan out of Never Land forever."

"Oh, if only I could fly!" he grumbled again, rubbing his chin with his hook. Suddenly his face brightened. He had an idea. He called for his first mate. "Smee, front and center! All hands on deck!" The pirate crew raced topside and stood at attention as Hook poured out the details of his scheme to take over Never Land.

Then they got busy. Some raced to find needles and thread. Some looked for green felt and glue. Smee searched for buttons. And Captain Hook hunched over his desk writing a note.

"My Dear Miss Bell," it read. "I would like so much to meet you. Please fly over Pirates Cove. I will be waiting." The note was signed, "Your Secret Admirer."

Tinker Bell jingled merrily when she read the note, which had been posted on Hangman's Tree. Someone wanted to meet her. Who could it be? She knew she should wait

until Peter came back so she could show him the note. But what harm could come from a quick flight over Pirates Cove to see who her admirer might be?

Leaving the note behind, Tinker Bell darted off to Pirates Cove. She flew across it three times, but saw no trace of a secret admirer. She saw nothing but the pirate ship. Surely her admirer wasn't a pirate! Then she glanced down, and to her surprise, saw Peter Pan tied to the mast of the ship. That note had been a trick!

Tinker Bell dove down to the rescue. She pulled up next to Peter and landed on his shoulder. But something wasn't right—this wasn't Peter Pan! It was a dummy made of cloth and green felt! Its button eyes stared at her.

Tinker Bell tried to take off again, but her feet were stuck. The dummy's shoulder was

covered with sticky glue! "Good day, Miss Bell," crooned Captain Hook, stepping out from behind a barrel. "We're so glad you could join us." Pirate laughter sounded from every quarter of the deck as the crew came out from their hiding places.

"I have a small favor to ask," Hook said. "Sprinkle my crew and ship with pixie dust so we can fly, won't you?" Tinker Bell jingled angrily and shook her head furiously, as if to say, "Never!"

Captain Hook pulled Tinker Bell free of the glue and shut her up in a ship's lantern. "There you'll stay, my little sprite, until you've changed your mind!" he sneered.

Back at Hangman's Tree, Peter Pan was holding an emergency meeting with Wendy, John, Michael, and the Lost Boys.

"As you know," he began, "Tinker Bell is missing. Wendy found this note." And Peter read the note aloud.

"Who could her secret admirer be?" asked Wendy. "Do you think she went to find out?"

"I don't know, but I'll bet Captain Hook is behind all this," said Peter. "I'm going to fly out to the pirate ship to investigate."

"That could be dangerous," warned John. "Let us go with you."

"No! It's better if I go alone," said Peter. "Without Tinker Bell, there's no way you could fly with me. You'd have to go in boats. The pirates would see us coming."

"But, Peter!" said Wendy. "If you do find Tinker Bell, you can't fight a ship full of

what we can do with it, but we'll take it along just in case.'' He passed the jar to Wendy for safekeeping.

While Peter Pan put his rescue plan in motion, Captain Hook was becoming frustrated. How could he get Tinker Bell to pixie-dust his crew? Threats of no food didn't work. He wasn't even sure what pixies ate. The threat of solitary confinement seemed much to her liking since it meant no visiting with the pirate crew.

Then Hook had a brainstorm. When he pointed out how badly things would go for Peter Pan if he were captured trying to rescue her, Tinker Bell gave in. She nodded her head and jingled sadly.

''Smee! Front and center!'' Hook loudly ordered.

Tinker Bell sprinkled the first mate with lots of pixie dust. ''Now for the test!'' crowed Hook, and he heaved Smee overboard to see if he could fly. A large splash of water washed over the deck. ''Man overboard!'' yelled Smee, and the pirates threw him a line and pulled him back on board.

''Why didn't he fly?'' cried Captain Hook. Then he remembered.

pirates alone. You'll need our help.'' Peter thought for a minute. He knew Wendy was right—but without Tinker Bell, there was no way to make Wendy and the boys fly. He would have to go alone.

''Wait a minute,'' Peter said. ''I have just the thing—something I've been saving a long, long time, for an emergency like this.''

Peter opened a small cupboard and took out two small, dusty jars. One was marked ''Pixie Dust,'' the other, ''Troll Dust.''

''Now watch this,'' he said, unscrewing the lid of the jar marked ''Fairy Dust.'' He sprinkled a tiny bit on John. John disappeared. A few minutes later he blinked back into view.

''What happened?'' asked Wendy.

Peter explained. ''This is pixie dust. Sprinkle it on and you disappear for a few minutes. We can use it to get to the pirate ship without being seen.''

''What about troll dust?'' asked John. ''May I try some of that, too?''

''It can be dangerous stuff,'' Peter warned. ''It can turn you to stone and it takes much longer to wear off. I don't know

"Try again," he ordered. "This time think happy thoughts. You have to think happy thoughts, or the pixie dust won't work."

Smee really tried hard to think a happy thought as Tinker Bell kept sprinkling, but his feet remained firmly planted on the deck.

"If you don't think a happy thought, you'll go overboard again, and this time no one will pull you out!" roared Hook. He was furious.

Suddenly an umbrella hit the pirate captain over the head. John suddenly popped into sight, holding on tight to the handle.

Then Peter Pan appeared overhead on the mast.

"Ahoy, Hook!" he shouted, leaping onto the deck in front of the captain and brandishing his dagger. "Prepare to do battle!" And Peter sliced the big feather off Captain hook's hat.

The fight was on. Boys began appearing all over the deck waving sticks and toy swords. John bonked another pirate with his umbrella as Little Michael hit him in the knees with his teddy bear.

While the battle raged, Wendy freed Tinker Bell from her lantern prison and handed her the bottle of troll dust. The little pixie jingled happily. She knew just what to do. She flew from one end of the ship to the other, spreading a thick cloud of troll dust over everyone.

Wendy looked on in horror. "You've sprinkled them all!" she gasped. "They'll all turn to stone!" Then she heard Peter's laugh as he stepped from the cloud. One by one everyone else was accounted for, too.

"You see," Peter explained, "just as pixie dust can only work if you are thinking happy thoughts, troll dust can only work when you are thinking mean thoughts. So the only ones who turned to stone were the pirates."

Wendy breathed a sigh of relief. Tinker Bell sprinkled everyone with pixie dust and they all flew back to Hangman's Tree for a big celebration.

And what happened to Captain Hook and his crew? Well, the last we knew, he was hard at work on still another scheme to take over Never Land. Do you think he'll ever succeed?

MADAM, I'M ADAM

What do the following words have in common with each other?

MOM, EYE, SEES, LEVEL, REDDER

What do these words have in common with the title of this article?

All are palindromes. A palindrome is a word, phrase, or sentence that reads the same forward and backward. Read the title from left to right. Then, from right to left. It says the same thing both ways: "Madam, I'm Adam." (When reading a palindrome backward, you may have to re-arrange the punctuation.)

Many people greatly enjoy palindromes—both collecting them and inventing them. They even make up crossword puzzles in which the answers to the clues are palindromes. Try to guess the one-word palindromes that these clues define:

1. The middle of the day
2. Male parent
3. Young dog
4. Female sheep

In many two-word palindromes, each of the words forms the other word when the letters are reversed. For example:

POOL LOOP
TOP POT
STRAW WARTS

In other two-word palindromes, you must change the spacing between letters when you read them backward:

Senile Felines

112

Panda here had nap

TIP IT
STOP SPOTS
SENILE FELINES

Here are some three- and four-word palindromes that use both techniques:

MAY SEES YAM
PAT DID TAP
POOR DOG, GO DROOP
NEVER ODD OR EVEN
TEN AT A NET
PANDA HERE HAD NAP

The longer the palindrome, the more difficult it is to create. The best method is to start with a word that can be written backward. Place it at the beginning and end of the palindrome, leaving lots of space in between:

PAM . . . . MAP

Now try using various words in the middle until you come up with a phrase or sentence:

PAM SAW RADAR WAS MAP
or
PAM SEES NEIL, AN ALIEN SEES MAP

People's names, particularly those that end with vowels, are often useful in creating palindromes:

NORMA, I AM RON
IMA! NO LEMON, NO MELON AM I!

It's fun making up a story to go along with the palindrome. When would a person insist he was neither a lemon nor a melon?

Make up stories—ludicrous, serious, or mysterious—for these palindromes:

BOB SAW RATS. STAR WAS BOB.
MA'S PALS SLAP SAM.
NO, IT IS OPEN ON ONE POSITION.

Some palindromes are famous. One of the best-known is "ABLE WAS I ERE I SAW ELBA." This refers to the famous French ruler Napoleon I, who was sent to the island of Elba after he was forced to abdicate in 1814. He later escaped from Elba and tried once again to rule Europe, but he was defeated by the British and their allies at the Battle of Waterloo.

Another famous palindrome is "A MAN, A PLAN, A CANAL: PANAMA." It most probably refers to Ferdinand de Lesseps, the 19th-century French engineer who made the first attempt to build a canal across the Isthmus of Panama.

There's even a palindrome that can be made almost infinitely long:

NEVER EVER EVER EVER EVER EVEN

You can keep inserting "ever" forever, and this will continue to be a palindrome. But no matter how long you make it, it must always have a beginning and an end, so that it can be read from either direction.

Pam sees Neil, an alien sees map

DOING WHAT COMES NATURALLY

When you come home from school, your dog runs to greet you, jumping up and licking your face. When you go out, it howls for hours—and all your neighbors complain.

Your cat doesn't seem to care very much whether you're home or not. Sometimes it's affectionate, curling up next to you and purring warmly. At other times, it's not so sweet—like the time it ripped the living room drapes to shreds with its claws.

What makes cats and dogs act the way they do? The answer lies in their natures. Their behavior—which may seem strange or funny to you—is natural and right to them. After all, our pet cats and dogs are descended from wild animals. While life with people has changed them in many ways, their instincts aren't all that different from those of their wild relatives.

ALL IN THE FAMILY

No matter how much you train your pets, a cat will never act like a dog, and a dog will never act like a cat. Most dogs want company, and they thrive on affection. They worship their owners, and they're always looking for a kind word and a pat. Cats, on the other hand, seem to regard their owners as equals. They like to play and be stroked, but they're also content to spend long periods of time alone.

The lives of wild dogs and cats provide a clue to these differences in nature. In the wild, wolves and dogs hunt in packs. They are runners who exhaust their prey in a long chase and then bring it down in a final group effort. Each wolf pack has a strict social order, or hierarchy. The pack leader is usually the biggest, strongest, smartest male; all the other wolves hold positions below him.

You can see how this way of life affects the way a dog behaves when it lives with a human family. The family takes the place of the pack, and the dog feels insecure when it's left alone. The dog also works out its spot in the social hierarchy of the "pack"—

usually at or near the bottom. In most cases, the dog decides that one of the adults in the family is the pack leader. That's why dogs are always looking up to people and hoping for approval—they need to belong.

In contrast, cats in the wild hunt alone. (Lions, who hunt in small groups called prides, are an exception.) Rather than chasing its prey, a cat stalks it quietly, unseen, and then springs at the last minute. This kind of hunting is best done alone—lots of cats stalking the same prey would make too much noise. And the cat's powerful forelegs and sharp claws permit it to bring down prey without help.

Thus a domestic cat doesn't feel as dependent on people as a dog does. People may be its friends, but the cat won't feel insecure when it's left alone. And it has no need to win approval from its human family.

Many other things that cats and dogs do can also be traced back to their ancestors' lives in the wild. A lone wolf will howl to find his pack—if the others hear the howling, they'll howl back. In the same way, your dog may howl when it's left alone. Many dogs also love to dig, in the flower garden or wherever they find loose dirt. Digging is an important skill for wild dogs and wolves. They may dig to find small burrowing animals, and they dig underground dens in which to raise their young.

Barking at (and even biting) strangers is another natural behavior for dogs. Wolf packs establish territories and keep out all strange wolves. Your dog establishes a territory, too. It may include your yard or the whole block, but the dog will bark at any stranger who enters it. Dogs and wolves mark the boundaries of their territories with scent marks, made by urinating on bushes, trees, and posts. When you take your dog for a walk and it sniffs each bush you pass, it's reading the "calling cards" left by other dogs.

Cats also establish territories and mark their boundaries with scent. A domestic cat may "own" an area from one third of a mile to three miles across. Whether or not the cat fights to defend its territory depends on how aggressive it is. But cats usually save their hissing and fighting for other cats—they rarely consider people to be intruders.

In the wild, cats are efficient hunters. But when a domestic cat catches a mouse or another small creature, it will often play with it —flipping it about with its paws for quite a while before making the kill. Scientists who study animals say this is because the cat is just working off its pent-up hunting energy.

Cats scratch to keep their claws sharp. Sharp claws are essential for hunting and also for climbing—something else a cat does with ease. In the wild, cats will use a tree

It's instinctive for cats to hiss and dogs to bark. Usually, they're just defending their territories.

Cats scratch and dogs dig. In the wild, cats need sharp claws for hunting and climbing, and dogs dig to find burrowing animals or to make underground dens.

trunk for claw-sharpening. But unless your house cat has a scratching post, it may use your furniture.

Cats are also known for two other traits: cleanliness and curiosity. They groom themselves for hours with their forepaws and tongues, and they bury their wastes neatly in a litterbox. In the wild, both these habits help prevent parasites and disease. Curiosity

is also an advantage for cats in the wild—being sharp observers and investigators helps cats avoid danger and find prey.

Both cats and dogs love to play, and that's another trait that serves their relatives well in the wild. Through play, young wolves and wild cats learn to hunt. And domestic cats and dogs work out their hunting instincts through play. Dogs love to chase balls (and sometimes cars), and cats love to stalk and pounce on their toys.

With so many instincts governing their behavior, how is it that cats and dogs have learned to live with people? One reason is another trait dogs and cats share: a long socialization period. The socialization period is the time when young animals learn who they are and how to behave, by copying the older animals around them. In many species, the young are socialized within hours or days of birth. But for cats and dogs, the socialization period doesn't even begin until a few weeks after they're born. And it continues until they're ten or twelve weeks old. So pups and kittens who grow up with people learn how to behave in a human household.

BODY TALK

Cats and dogs have dozens of ways to tell us how they feel and what they think. But their ways of communicating are sometimes quite different.

Both animals communicate dominance and submission through eye contact. If you meet your pet's gaze, who looks away first? Whoever stares longest is top dog (or cat). Don't try this with a strange dog, though. Dogs sometimes interpret a long stare as a threat and may attack as a result. If you meet a strange dog that may be aggressive, avoid eye contact altogether. But don't run away —that would tell the dog that you're afraid.

Body position also helps tell you whether an animal is feeling submissive or aggressive. A dog may roll over on its back to show submission; that's its way of saying "you're the boss." If the dog thinks *it's* the boss, it may jump up and put its paws on your shoulders. If a dog is aggressive, it will often stand with ears and tail perked up and its hackles —the hairs on its back—raised. The raised hackles make the dog seem larger to its opponent. When the dog is ready to fight, it may lower its head to protect its throat.

Cats also fluff up their fur—all over their bodies and even on their tails—to look larger to an opponent. When they're afraid or worried, they sit with their tails curled around their bodies. When they're *very* frightened, they arch their backs and hold their tails straight up in a "Halloween cat" pose. But a cat that brushes against your leg and arches its back usually just wants to be petted.

If the cat rubs your leg with its head and tail, it's marking you with scent that says you're a friend. A cat may also pat your face with its paw to show friendship—with its claws carefully retracted, of course. A dog that wants to show friendship will lick you, especially on the face.

Tails are great indicators of mood. When a dog is frightened or ashamed, it tucks its tail between its legs. A level, wagging tail is a sign of happy friendship. But be careful if the tail is carried high, even if it's still wagging—the dog may be showing aggression. Cats twitch their tails when they're annoyed and when they're stalking prey—even if the prey is just a scrap of paper or a rubber mouse.

When your cat wants to play, it may lie on its side and bat the air with its paws. Your dog may nudge you with its nose, raise a paw, or crouch down in front with its hindquarters raised. Dogs also have a "play face"—a silly sort of grin—that they put on when they want to romp.

Cats and dogs can also produce a whole range of vocal expressions to tell you how they feel. Dogs whine and whimper to show submission or to get attention, bark when they're happy or excited, yelp when they're hurt, and snarl and growl when they want to make a threat. Cats meow when they want attention—or food—but they rarely meow to each other. They may chatter when they spot a bird and yowl when they gather outside at night. And they hiss and spit to show anger. People don't know exactly why cats purr, but it's usually connected with the pleasure of being petted or groomed.

Once you understand why your pet does the things it does and what it's trying to tell you through its body language and the sounds it makes, you'll enjoy your pet more. And you may be better able to keep it from doing the wrong (but natural) things—like howling all day or shredding the drapes.

To show trust, friendliness, and affection, a dog will lick your face, and a cat will brush its body up against you.

ART NOUVEAU
ART DECO

Art Nouveau and Art Deco are two styles of art design that were very popular in the early part of the 20th century. Today they are in demand once again.

The Victorian era, from the mid- to late 1800's, was a time of tradition and "proper" social values. Art, architecture, and the decorative arts (such as furnishings, fabrics, and jewelry) were traditional and proper, too. But by the end of the period, many people had decided that styles were too traditional —even stuffy.

And so something of a revolution swept through Europe and North America. But it wasn't a political revolution—it was a revolution in art design. Designers broke loose from the old styles, producing free, flowing, natural forms. The style known as art nouveau (from the French words for "new art") was born. At the height of its popularity, the art nouveau influence could be seen in everything from clothing to buildings.

By the 1920's, however, the curving lines that had at first seemed so free and new had become as old-hat as their Victorian predecessors. Designers reacted again, producing another new style—art deco—which relied on blocky, geometric forms.

Today neither style is the rage it once was, but both have undergone revivals in popularity. The art nouveau and art deco designs produced in the early part of the century are in demand again. And the two styles have also influenced contemporary designs.

ART NOUVEAU

France was the major center of the art nouveau movement. But the movement had actually begun in England and spread from there to the continent of Europe and the United States.

Several different influences came together to produce art nouveau. Earlier styles that also emphasized curving lines—such as the rococo, Gothic, and early Celtic styles— were revived and rediscovered in the late 1800's. There were also new influences. Japanese prints, for example, became popular in Western countries. Their flowing forms and flat (rather than three-dimensional) portrayals of objects affected many painters of the time.

In part, art nouveau was an outgrowth of these styles. But there was also something different about it: In art nouveau, for the first time, the most important aspect of a work of art was its design—not its subject matter or the emotions it produced.

This was the philosophy of William Morris, a leader in the English arts and crafts movement. Morris was dismayed by the ugliness of new products being produced by factories—a result of the Industrial Revolution. Morris wanted artisans to produce handmade items and stressed that beautiful designs should be part of everyday life. His designs and his philosophy had an important effect on art nouveau designers and artists.

Art nouveau designers preferred to start with forms from nature—especially anything that curved. Leaves and flowers, swans and peacocks, flowing water, and the human body were favorite subjects. But natural forms weren't simply copied. The artist would twist, bend, and distort them to make his design, sometimes until they were hardly recognizable. Some artists went a step further, working completely in geometric shapes and abstract patterns.

Art nouveau illustrators, such as Aubrey Beardsley of England and the Czech painter and decorator Alphonse Mucha, created works that were two-dimensional, with little background or sense of depth. Often figures were merely silhouettes, and often the pictures were created in simple, flat colors or in black and white. Lines were the most important features of these works—sweeping, swirling lines that suggested action and tension.

Architecture, of course, required three dimensions. But even here, the art nouveau style emphasized lines. Decorative swirls and curved windows covered the outsides of buildings. Entrances were outlined with twisting wrought-iron archways. Among the most famous of such designs are the entrances to the Métro (the Paris subway), designed by Hector Guimard around the turn of the century.

Despite the fanciful exteriors, however, the emphasis in an art nouveau building was on the inside. Everything from wall paneling and furniture to silverware and fabric was designed to harmonize with the new style. Glass in glowing colors—in stained-glass windows and lampshades and in hand-blown vases—was often featured. The glass designs of Louis Tiffany of the United States are among the most famous of the time.

Art nouveau designers achieved some of their wildest flights of fancy in jewelry. In

signers called the Glasgow School, who had used patterns of horizontal and vertical lines in their work, were especially influential.

Other sources for the new style were the arts and architecture of ancient Egypt and the Aztecs, which relied heavily on massive geometric forms such as the pyramid. Exotic, richly colored stage designs for the ballet and theater also had an effect. And so did the development of cubism and similar movements in art, which broke subjects down into basic geometric elements.

The new style was also influenced by a change in philosophy. Rather than glorifying handmade items, the designers of this time wanted to create things that could be mass-produced by machine—to join art and industry. The idea was to make good design available to everyone, not just the wealthy.

This new art style was called art deco—its name came from an exhibition of decorative

place of the traditional gold, silver, and diamonds of Victorian days, jewelers made use of pearls, coral, opals, and even glass, set in bronze, brass, and aluminum. With these gems and settings, jewelers created glittering serpents and peacocks and twisting leaves and flowers. French designer René Lalique was particularly renowned for his exotic work in jewelry and glassware.

In time, however, the once-fresh lines of art nouveau became excessive, as though each design were trying to outdo the one before. One critic termed the movement a "strange decorative disease." People were ready for a change.

ART DECO

For a while, people went back to earlier styles, those that had been popular in the 1700's. But after World War I, a new style began to develop. Like art nouveau, it grew out of many different sources.

One source was art nouveau itself, especially in its more restrained and geometric forms. A turn-of-the-century group of de-

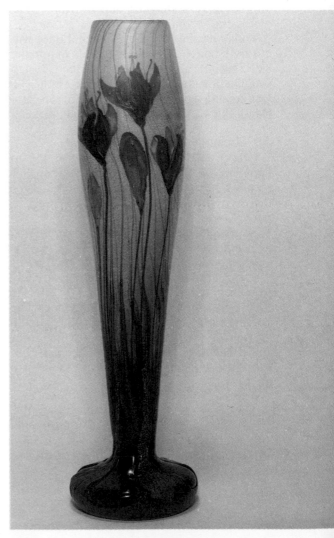

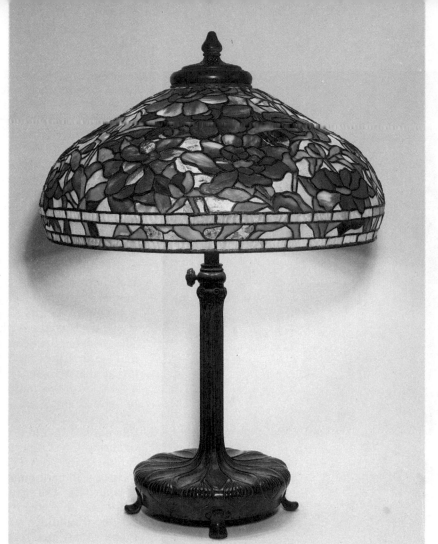

Art Nouveau: flowing, curving lines; natural forms—leaves and flowers, butterflies and peacocks; decorative and ornate objects; fine woods, semiprecious gems, and bronze and brass; hand-blown vases and brilliantly colored stained-glass lamps.

121

arts in Paris in 1925. Art deco designs were symmetrical (balanced) and solid-looking. They used rectangles and similar shapes in preference to curves and twisting lines. And they made use of the materials of mass-production—plastic, glass, concrete, and chrome.

Like the illustrations in the art nouveau style, those of art deco were often two-dimensional, in black and white or simple but vibrant colors. They were also highly stylized. But there the similarities ended. The forms in art deco pictures seem massive and solid. Lines are bold and straight, joining at sharp angles. Often the pictures have a dark, brooding atmosphere; they show man in the machine age.

In architecture, art deco could be given full play. Blocklike concrete buildings and towering skyscrapers, such as the Chrysler Building in New York City, echoed the forms of ancient buildings. The top of a skyscraper, for example, might stair-step to a point like an Aztec pyramid. The outsides of art deco buildings were vastly simpler than those of art nouveau buildings. Still, they were often decorated with geometric carvings and sculpture.

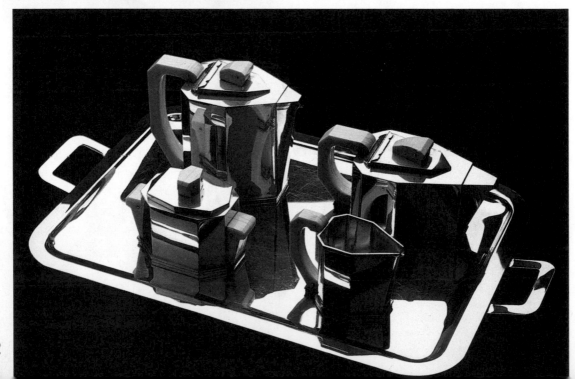

Inside, the decoration echoed the geometric forms and blocklike shapes. Like art nouveau, art deco stressed the importance of design. But a principle important to art deco designers was that objects should be functional—that is, they should look like what they were, and they should be designed so that they would be easy to use. Thus most chairs, tables, teapots, and other household objects were simple. Tubular steel was often used in the making of furniture, and chrome and plastic were used for smaller objects.

At the height of its popularity, in the 1930's, the art deco style could be seen everywhere. Jewelry was designed in blocky shapes or in patterns that reflected the art of ancient Egypt. Pottery and glassware stressed geometric forms and bright, vibrant colors. Even plastic radios were styled in the stair-step shape of Aztec pyramids.

As was the case with art nouveau, however, many people found that the art deco style had gone too far. Much of what was produced didn't reflect good design. Gradually, art deco was discarded in favor of newer styles.

Today people have come to appreciate both art nouveau and art deco once again. And they recognize the important step these styles took in breaking with the traditional designs of the past. By developing new, bold ways of presenting lines and shapes and by stressing the importance of good design, art nouveau and art deco laid the groundwork for contemporary design.

INDEX

ILLUSTRATION CREDITS
AND ACKNOWLEDGMENTS